A LIFETIME OF BADGERS

A Lifetime of
BADGERS

Peter Hardy

DAVID & CHARLES

NEWTON ABBOT   LONDON

NORTH POMFRET (VT)   VANCOUVER

To JSH 1955–68

ISBN 0 7153 6804 4

Library of Congress Catalog Card No 74-20462

Set in 12 on 13pt Bembo and printed in
Great Britain by Latimer Trend & Company Ltd Plymouth
for David & Charles (Holdings) Limited
South Devon House Newton Abbot Devon

Published in the United States of America
by David & Charles Inc
North Pomfret Vermont 05053 USA

Published in Canada by Douglas David & Charles Limited
132 Philip Avenue North Vancouver BC

CONTENTS

		Page
	Preface	9
1	The Animal	11
2	Senses and Survival	23
3	The Badger's Year	36
4	Subsistence and Health	52
5	The Sett	73
6	Distribution and Population	87
7	An Ancient Briton: The Badger in Myth, History and Literature	102
8	Watching Badgers	117
9	Brock Triumphant?	128
	Appendix: The Protection of Badgers	137
	References	141
	Acknowledgements	143
	Index	145

LIST OF ILLUSTRATIONS

	Page
A badger's head with distinctive markings (*J. Allan Cash*)	25
Sow badger caught in snare	25
Beginning a badger dig (*J. Griffith*)	26
Terriers baiting their prey (*J. Griffith*)	26
A dew-soaked cub	27
Testing the air	28
A female badger with bedding	28
The first emergence	61
A typical sett	61
Seven-month-old cubs at play	62
Boar and sow grooming each other	62
An energetic scratch	63
Two views of badger skull (*Peter Hardy*)	64
The south Asian hog badger (*London Zoo*)	64
Badger on well-used track	89
Tree used as playground	89

A hole in constant use (*Peter Hardy*)   90

Tree used as scratching post   90

Kim, a domesticated young sow (*Peter Hardy*)   107

Mature male (*N. Clark*)   107

Family group (*Geoffrey Wright*)   108

Muddy badger excavating   108

All photographs by P. Bennett except where credited

PREFACE

Perhaps it might be considered odd that a politician should have the sort of interest which demands periods of personal silence and a degree of isolation. I hope, though, that my constituents in Rother Valley will agree that I make a sufficient noise elsewhere so that an occasional evening hour or two by a badger sett is not begrudged.

There may be the view, of course, that it is even more strange that a South Yorkshireman from what is regarded as an area of heavy industry should be at all interested in badgers. The fact is that, whilst my constituency is much concerned with coal and steel, there is a lot of wooded and open country within it. Further, there is a long and wholesome tradition that mining folk have a concern for nature and the countryside. Most of our people are not at all remote from field and woodland. Discussing civil service dispersal last year I was able to emphasise that our environment was not quite so dreadful as is sometimes supposed. I quoted the fact that kingfishers breed within it as well as badgers.

Sometimes after visiting a local sett I notice the glow of the lights of nearby Sheffield in the night sky. Other steel towns like Rotherham are close by, too, and yet there is still an abundance of birds and many beasts, trees and wild flowers around me. Possibly most of these are there despite man and often unremarked by him. One hopes that this quite rich diversity of life will be maintained whether lack of awareness continues or not.

I am pleased that I was able to play a part in securing the passage of the Badgers Act through the House of Commons in 1973. I believe that this measure of protection was essential for, just as the lover of natural history enjoys greater access and opportunity for the indulging of interest, so also do others of our species which can be the most dangerous and destructive of all predators.

For too long man maintained an attitude towards badgers which was unjustified, being more related to medieval superstition than to reality. Thus, for centuries there has been persecution, often quite barbaric in character. That should now cease for, not before time, this animal is covered by protective legislation which might well be regarded as a model for the future conservation of species.

The badger is held in increasingly high esteem. The Forestry Commission offered it protection from two years ago. The County Naturalists' Trusts chose the badger's head as their emblem before that. Their's was an appropriate selection for, as well as being among the oldest, the badger is possibly the most fascinating of all our wild mammals.

Parliament has now confirmed the increased approval generally afforded to the badger. A real measure of legal protection is established. One hopes that persecution is over and done with at last. It would be interesting to note whether this will bring Brock above ground a little earlier in the evening!

CHAPTER I

THE ANIMAL

Three disreputable men leave an elderly van by a hedge and walk unhurriedly into nearby woodland. They carry sacks, spades and a long-handled implement. Yapping terriers sniff about their heels. The dogs are excited. One of the men shouts, another curses and the dogs are quiet, sitting or lying, still but utterly watchful as the intruders approach some holes in the slightly sloping ground. Leading from the holes are heaps or ridges of bare earth which have been displaced by excavation. Some of these ridges are quite high, stretching five or six feet from the holes.

A terrier is picked up, head and tail, and placed in the entrance of one of the holes. The dog needs little urging to descend, its short tail quivering. One man kneels attentively at the entrance. The others take their spades and move short distances from the hole. They, too, put their heads close to the ground, listening. Suddenly, one of them points to the ground. After a brief conversation the two furthest from the hole begin digging furiously at the selected spot. Soon a substantial amount of soil has been piled behind them. Occasionally, the man at the entrance calls out to the dog below. Every few minutes all the men appear to listen carefully. The first dog re-appears, blood upon the white of its head coming from an ear which is freshly torn. The second terrier disappears down the entrance hole, and later a third dog is sent below. The men continue digging so that their trenching grows wider and is steadily deepened.

Soon the men lay aside their spades. One seizes the long-handled implement whilst another speaks to the terriers underground. The long-handled implement is taken. At one end are tongs or clamps which are pushed towards movement at the side of the newly-dug trench. The handles are parted and then closed again. The man holding the tool pushes whilst the other bends and takes hold of the terrier now snarling in excited fury.

Suddenly with a jerked and turning motion the man with the tongs moves and straightens. Gripped in the clamp is a bulky-bodied grey and black animal, hair bristling, teeth bared in a fierce terror. It writhes against the metal clutch. All the terriers rush yapping, snarling, teeth snapping. Two of them jump and close teeth upon the suspended form.

The captured animal is pushed into a sack which is closed and tied before the bundle is pushed to one side. Life within the sack moves a little. Some noise can be heard from it. The terriers rush at it snarling eagerly. The bundle moves more and the terriers worry at it briefly before the men drive them off. Once more the digging is resumed.

Later, in a deserted old quarry, both men and dogs gather around a low enclosure. The sack can be seen lying on the floor of the same old van. One of the men picks up the tongs and pokes into the neck of the sack. He steps back, arms and handles extended. At the end of the tool, again, the grey animal writhes, hair stiffened out. Someone takes a length of chain from the van and ties it around the animal's hind quarters.

A great din ensues, the deep low sound of the animal just distinguishable from the yapping fury of the terriers. The man with the tongs releases one handle and the chained captive falls to the ground as the dogs rush in. The muddled battle appears to take a motion, an existence, of its own. Occasionally some of the terriers dance back and their enemy is more isolated in vision, chained, for a moment still, unable to move far, but its head is low down and it is capable of fighting on.

One of the men pushes the dogs aside and kicks out into the grey creature. The dogs pour back raging upon it. Now blood is more obvious but the fighting continues. One, and then a second of the dogs is picked up injured and pushed aside to be enleashed. Eventually someone picks up a spade, swings it high and brings it down metal edge hard into the shape which jerks at the impact. Soon the grey bundle is still and silent, wet, bedraggled and lifeless. Now the terriers growl even more and worry at the bloodied carcass, which is now torn, soiled with froth and dirt.

So a badger dies.

There are other ways of seeing the badger.

A wood is scarcely silent. Even when the wind is barely detectable there is some sound, some motion which creates noise. Outside the wood tranquillity may be equally rare. A peaceful evening will have some continuing or persistent break in its calmness, although it may only be of rustles and soft murmurings. In the distance a farm vehicle is perhaps working, whilst a car drones out of earshot along roads which are never far away.

There are moments, however, when there is at least the impression of silence, accompanied by the depth if not the solemnity of Wordsworth's pervasive harmony. On such a night it seems fitting that a badger's emergence from below ground should be noiseless and unheralded. Whenever it appears in a hushed evening it provides a surprise—surprise which affects even an experienced watcher and may astonish those who have rarely encountered the animal before.

Only a minority of people have seen a wild badger even though this animal often lives very close to man. Certainly badgers live sufficiently near to die upon our roads in considerable numbers. These road casualties provide many people with their only direct observation of the animal, a fleeting glimpse of a carcass upon a busy road.

There is a freshness about every witnessed emergence; the old novelty is never entirely lost even though the experience may have been repeated a score, or a hundred times before. The surprise seems greater when emergence is sudden. Often, though, the surfacing involves a much more protracted procedure. A head is glimpsed at the entrance. There is a long and careful savouring of the air, and possibly the murmur of cubs eager for play. Or there may be nothing seen but a grunt heard or the scratch of a stone in a deep entrance.

Eventually, though, the badger will appear. Usually, there is sufficient daylight left to allow it to be observed quite clearly. For the new watcher the first impressions are quite dominated by the visual impact of the head or by the fact that the animal is larger than most people imagine.

The badger is not a merely pretty animal, nor one of ostentatious elegance, but it is handsome. First, the eye is drawn to the two black stripes, distinctive upon the white background of the head. These stripes stretch from the neck almost to the nostrils. Narrower at the front, they broaden out to almost a couple of inches' width before the small dark eyes which are set inside the stripes. The ears, black but with white tips, also stand within the stripes, placed quite wide apart so that the head does not appear to be weak or insubstantial.

In the twilight the badger's body is less striking, not being sharply outlined. It is bulky, an animal which is neither delicate in its construction nor too elegant upon its strong, rather short legs. This low-leggedness is emphasised by the badger's colouring, by its thickish coat and, possibly, by the short tail which may be no more than 5in long. The tail is said to be a pointer to the animal's sex in that a somewhat slimmer, more pointed-tailed badger may be a female whilst a spatulate tail is likely to be a boar's. I do not know whether this characteristic is absolutely invariable but it seems to be a frequent one.

The animal as a whole presents a rather large and solid appearance, suggesting a certain ponderance of manner which may explain the fable and story personification of the badger as a respectable creature, conscious of its dignity but decent in its intent. However, whilst the badger may be described as ponderous and ungainly it can move with some silent speed and smooth agility. It is not normally given to really rapid motion for, man and his creatures apart, no other animal in Britain will come into conflict with a badger from choice. Thus, it is that the normal gait is one of a rather rolling nonchalance, and away from the sett it often pays little heed to observers. Indeed, it can and does make a surprising amount of noise as it moves through a wood.

The feet are wide and the badger walks upon the full foot so that in normal gait the track reveals an even tread with the five toes marked in symmetrical pattern. It is possible to gain some idea of the size of the badger's feet by comparing its tracks with those of the fox which appear very much smaller. Unfortunately, the tracks are not usually clear for in normal walk the hind foot is placed over the print of the front foot. Enough can be seen, though, to appreciate the comparative size of the badger's feet which are specially adapted to carry out one of the badger's main and instinctive activities, digging.

The animal digs to establish its home and much of its food is obtained through digging, too. More effort is required and somewhat greater use is made of the front feet than the hind, although the latter are used often in a combined earth-moving operation with front and back limbs in complementary activity. Strong and sizeable, the badger's claws are kept in even condition, long but not very sharp, by normal digging. The claws are not retractable but generally extend further than the claws of most mammals appear to do.

Of course, the badger is not a slight animal. Size varies immensely, the boar usually weighing up to 30lb. A mature male is often heavier, especially by late summer when it is likely to be 3 or 4lb more than at the end of a severe winter. Weights of

40lb or over have been recorded, the heaviest actually measured being 43lb.[29] Exceptional weights have been claimed for badgers in the Scottish highlands where it is said that this animal, like the hill fox, is heavier than the lowland creature which has not had to withstand the same extremes of climate and hardship. However, the latest record I have noted is of a wild English boar of 37lb in 1973.[18]

Generally the sow is 3 or 4lb lighter than the boar, and an inch or two less than his nose-to-tail length of about 3ft. The ancient measurement, one yard, is most appropriately regarded as the standard length of a badger, one of our oldest wild creatures. Standing not much more than a foot high at the shoulders, the badger is a substantial mammal with a low centre of gravity, not easily overwhelmed.

Centuries ago the badger was often called a 'grey' and the body usually does present an appearance of overall greyness. This is due largely to the fact that on much of the animal each hair is both black and white in colouring. The hairs on the upper parts of the neck and body, and on the sides, are white or yellow near the skin and at the tips and black, sometimes shading to brown, in between. Often as a badger grows older the dark band in the middle of the hair shrinks a little so that the overall impression may be somewhat paler. On a youngster, possibly a quarter of each of these hairs is black but this proportion might be reduced by one-third or so in old age. Sometimes, though, an older animal seems more brown.

On the lower and under parts the hair is very much darker. The legs and feet are usually black, possibly with brown or white markings on the feet, but the tail is light-coloured. This pattern of shading, dark below and paler above, is often encountered in nocturnal mammals, possibly so that the outline of the animal is not so sharply noticeable in darkness. However, despite the occasional suggestion that the badger's black and white head provides camouflage, in moonlight that feature is most conspicuous. A number of wild animals share this distinctive marking, and it is possible that it serves as a warning and identification.

Dr Ernest Neal has suggested that creatures with this distinctive head marking are actually quite formidable animals which possess a means of effective defence.[19] The skunk provides a most marked example of this characteristic.

We cannot be absolutely certain if there is an evolved value or purpose in the distinctive head. I strongly doubt if it does serve as a means of providing identification underground as was once thought. The stripes are very conspicuous above ground but it seems unlikely that they could be discerned inside the sett. In any case, the badger's hearing and scenting powers are keen enough to mean that visual recognition is quite unnecessary.

While almost all badgers have these distinctive head stripes there are some slight variations in length and pattern. Most variations are scarcely noticeable; even the fact that the stripes are dark brown rather than black may not be easily discerned in the dusk.

There can be much more obvious variety in body colour. Sometimes, if rarely, an albino appears. In this case, of course, the head stripes may be absent and there is absence of pigmentation so the eyes are pink. Such animals do not appear to be any less substantial in physique and they seem to be entirely accepted by other animals in their particular family or clan. However, conspicuity is inevitably a hazard to survival. Perhaps this is the reason for the comparative rarity of the albino in this species.

Frequently brown markings, usually of a chestnut shade, are found. This colour may occur most often in the head stripes or on the feet. In a description of a domesticated badger Mrs Sylvia Shepherd[26] noted that a visiting pet badger, a sow, had chestnut head markings and that her own boar developed chestnut stripes on his paws as he matured. These markings were described as being most prominent when the mating period occurred, a sign of the animal's sexual maturity.

I do not believe that all adults carry such markings but chestnut brown on head and feet are by no means rare. I suppose that it is unlikely that adequate research will ever be undertaken into the incidence of this or any other colour variation. If it were possible it may be that variation in the regional incidence of a particular coloration would be noted. The two badgers described by Mrs Shepherd were from the Lakeland area. In South Yorkshire, whilst I have seen chestnut markings on adult badgers, I could not claim that it is normally encountered. At the same time the comments by Dr Neal[19] do not suggest that such coloration is usual in the South West where there may possibly be a greater likelihood of a yellow colouring being encountered.

It was once suggested that the effect was caused by generations of badgers living in yellow soil. This seems most unlikely since not all badgers in such a sett may have this colouring. Dr Neal has recorded that he watched a yellow family when the two cubs were small. The sow was bright yellow, the boar less so and both cubs were yellow. The colour is obviously an inheritance from parents who themselves possess or transmit this trait. The same applies where the badger is of a darker brown colour, and brown or sandy-coloured (erythristic) badgers are not uncommon.

The comments made by Turberville in 1576[30] are rather interesting here. The theory was that there were two kinds of badgers, one resident in rocky areas, the other in more sandy soil. Turberville described the latter as 'badgerdwhelps' having higher legs and with nose, throat and ears of yellow. The yellow on these animals was said to be the colour of a marten's throat. The animals living in rocky areas he called 'badgerdpigs', and they were said to be more fierce and to 'stink worse' than their yellowed relatives. Turberville commented that neither sort kept company with the other.

Today we must regard these views as being false, as there seems to be neither zoological nor anatomical justification for Turberville's theory. The Elizabethan author also believed that the older the badger the greyer the coat, and that young animals are much whiter than the adults. This impression may have been caused by the fact that the cub's coat is a little softer and may look a little fluffier, whilst the head markings may appear just a shade less sharply distinct in the very early weeks of a cub's life.

When the cubs are born they seem rather dull in colour. In their early weeks the cubs' hair is quite soft and it is possibly only in early life that the coat of the British badger could be attractive or suitable for the fur trade. Soon the texture of the coat harshens and the normal fur of the carnivorous predator is produced. The full coat should consist of an undercoat of quite short hair much softer than the long outer hair which is strong and hard. In temperate regions the badger appears to possess only the stiff guard hairs of the outer coat.

Most carnivores in non-tropical areas appear to possess this type of coat. All the weasel family seem to be fur-bearing as are many breeds of dogs including the Spitz breeds like the Keeshond, the Samoyed and the Chow Chow.

The badger's coat is quite thick and since the hairs are harsh in texture it is able to withstand hard weather and, of course, the coat is likely to be at its most dense by the time winter is well advanced, after the new hair has replaced that shed in the autumnal moult. This shedding of old hair takes a month or more. The hair, as with most other mammals which change coats, is lost gradually, usually from the legs, shoulders and underparts first.

It is wrong to believe, as is often suggested, that the badger's coat offers it protection from insect infestation. It suffers from the normal parasite burden, one reason perhaps for the energetic grooming it performs. Whether this is of real assistance in promoting coat and skin health cannot be proven although without it the coat would be much less attractive and clean. This grooming activity does seem instinctive or at least learned at an early age by imitative practice, and the only really dirty badger I have ever seen was in captivity. Pet badgers taken into domesticity at a very early age have been known to attend to grooming and even to scratch the hair of members of the family with which they live.

A number of other references to Turberville's views will be

made and, whilst as has been indicated there is doubt about certain of the opinions quoted, there can be definite agreement with the view that the badger is a particularly tough and tenacious creature. Turberville regarded the badger as hard to kill. So it may seem to be.

Stories told then and since have referred to the apparent ineffectiveness of quite heavy blows delivered upon a badger's head. Given the force of such blows the animal's survival has seemed almost miraculous. However, there is a rather more mundane and physiological reason for this. Survival is due not to any power of wondrous magic but to the unique nature of the badger's skull. This is very solidly constructed and strengthened by a ridge of bone running centrally from over the neck to the middle of the skull.

The skull pictured on page 64 was collected from the carcass of a badger which lived in Yorkshire's most southerly sett. The animal died in May 1973. Its carcass lay about 30yd from the sett. Unfortunately the condition of the body was such that I did not closely examine it when I took the skull. However, it seems very likely that the animal was a female since the two cubs at the sett were accompanied by only one adult which appeared to be a boar.

This is rather circumstantial evidence, of course. However, the skull is not a large one and if one accepts the estimates of skull sizes by Mortimer Batten in 1923,[2] there are further grounds supporting the view that the skull belonged to a sow badger. Batten stated that the skull of a male badger is an average of $5\frac{1}{2}$in long whilst the length of the female skull is $5\frac{1}{4}$in. This skull is fractionally under the latter length and it is also of the same width as that given as the average for a female of $3\frac{1}{4}$in, one quarter of an inch less than the width of the skull of the male. Hence my belief that the skull illustrated is that of a female.

Badgers' skulls are not at all massive but examination shows that they are of considerable and robust strength. The central ridge of bone overhangs the base of the skull and so adds to its protective character. This ridge of bone is about a quarter of an inch deep, quite narrow but strong. At the centre of the head the height of the ridge reduces and it forks into two raised lips of bone, curving to the outside above the ears.

The skull is of mono-construction sloping downwards a little to the nose. Over the front of the nasal cavity it is much less substantial so that this is the only really vulnerable part of the head. A blow administered on the top of the head is likely to be quite ineffective, its force diverted away from the centre—the reason for the medieval wonderment.

Because of the shape and structures of the skull the jaw muscles have most secure anchorages, making it possible for the badger to deliver a comparatively powerful bite. The lower jaw itself is unusual, being almost enclosed in its joint, so that (in an adult) it cannot be dislocated unless there is severe damage to the skull itself. In the immature badger the two halves of the lower jaw are not always well fused. In the skull pictured these halves were separated so that we have further evidence that the sow was a comparatively young animal. Certainly if the cubs in the sett were hers then they must have been from her first and only litter.

In this skull the teeth are intact except for the two extremely tiny pre-molars in the lower jaw which had been lost. These are often lost before maturity is complete. The two even tinier vestigial pre-molars in the upper jaw of this skull are present and since these teeth and the rest appear to be in very wholesome condition there is further evidence that the animal was quite young.

The badger's full dental equipment consists of a total of 38 teeth, the incisors or front teeth close together and not at all large. In the lower jaw there are 6 of these, 2 canine teeth and 8 pre-molars, the first 2 of which are the extremely tiny vestigial teeth already mentioned. Then there are 4 molars, 2 on each side; the front ones of each pair are larger than the back two.

There are only 2 large molars in the upper jaw with 4 incisors, 2 canines and 6 pre-molars. Again, the front pair of these pre-molars are extremely tiny. The canine teeth, though, are large and powerful, deep rooted and typical of the carnivore. However, the size of the molars is such that the badger can deal with more than a fleshy diet. Although it does not eat with a chewing motion, the badger's teeth and jaws are strong and of such a character that it can crush a wide variety of foods including snails.

The badger cub produces a small set of first teeth, of appropriately small size, which appear to point forward. This must be regarded as convenient since the cubs may be feeding from the sow for quite a long time.

Many badgers lose one or more of their incisors at quite an early age. Not the most essential of teeth, the incisors complement rather than serve as essentials, even though some foods might well be taken more easily if a full set exists. Vestigial teeth apart, the incisors are almost certain to be the first to go but without these the badger can still consume a diverse diet.

This ability to consume a very wide range of food is of great importance to the badger which is not adequately equipped to pursue mobile living quarry. However, a sufficiency of food is obtainable through the use of a combination of its well developed sense of smell, the very strong feet and limbs so essential for digging and, of course, its teeth and jaws.

CHAPTER 2

SENSES AND SURVIVAL

It can be seen, then, that the badger possesses the characteristics of strength rather than speed; to be formidable rather than agile and, therefore, in the absence of predators capable of tackling its species—man apart—it is well suited for survival in our environment. It is fair to say that its evolutionary adaptation and genetic inheritance have been generally appropriate and successful.

This process of adaptation is no doubt continuing for in certain respects the changes seem incomplete. For example, the vestigial pre-molars may disappear in some future generation. Similarly there may be grounds to believe that the badger's power of vision has become less acute than it was in generations long ago. However, there is at least a possibility that the badger's sight is a little less used than it is usable.

Any experienced observer is aware that the badger relies much less upon vision than upon its senses of smell or hearing. Movement and conspicuously light colours or severe breaks in the outline of its immediate environment are usually detected but an immobile inconspicuous object, a person not revealing presence by smell or noise, will generally be ignored. This has led to the view that the badger's eyesight is extremely weak. Yet in recent years opinion has been advanced that it is the use of, or reliance upon, sight that is meagre rather than the actual power of vision.

Perhaps the badger relies less upon sight than those breeds of dog which are also 'nose specialists'. Some dogs for instance seem able to survive without heavy disadvantage despite deafness or, in some cases, blindness. One of my dogs would never markedly rely upon its hearing; scent or sight had to confirm aural evidence before a response was elicited—although it was not deaf. So it may be with the badger's eyes. Sight is far less powerful than the senses of smell or hearing and, therefore, reliance is upon those more powerful senses.

The badger's scenting powers are very strong. Some observers have realised that a scent can be noticed at a distance of at least 10yd, in a barely discernible wind. Certainly a badger can follow a recent trail without difficulty. Before leaving the sett its first action is not to look but to assess the air. In view of the sharpness of this sense it is not at all surprising that a nocturnal mammal like the badger should have become less than reliant upon its vision.

During my own observations, however, I have noticed that badgers do use their eyes as a confirmatory sense. On a number of occasions during the last ten years I have placed myself at distances of between five and fifteen yards from a sett with any wind, sometimes quite a strong wind, blowing towards me. Badgers have emerged there, as elsewhere, carefully using nose and ears to check security before fully surfacing. If there have been suspicions the badger has appeared rather more vigilant. On those occasions when I have worn dull sober clothing and stood with my back to a tree, or in any position where I did not really break the skyline or the outline to which the badger was accustomed, suspicion has not been confirmed and normal activity followed. But on those evenings when I have worn

Page 25 (*above*) The badger's distinctive head markings; (*below*) sow badger caught in snare

Page 26 (*above*) The beginning of a badger dig; (*below*) the terriers go to work, baiting the still live animal which stands no chance of reprieve

Page 27 A dew-soaked cub

Page 28 (*above*) Testing the air before emergence, with eyes almost closed; (*below*) a female badger dragging a pile of fresh bedding to the entrance of the sett

light-coloured clothing or when I have stood in a conspicuous position then the badger's suspicions have not been soothed; it has stared towards me and often returned underground for a while. In those cases I believe that the eyes have noticed cause for concern but before action was stimulated confirmation of danger from other senses was required.

This seems to be supported by the conclusions of J. F. Wilson who suggests that the badger's eyes are not adapted to nocturnal activity so that it does not possess the night vision which has evolved in certain species.[32] Perhaps, in an evolutionary sense, the badger has not been a night forager for a long time. Mr Wilson also makes the point that, since the badger's nose is kept within a foot or so of the ground, the eyes are focused upon close objects so that retinal images further away cannot be clear at all as a result of the pattern of focal habit.

This theory could be developed to the point where it could be claimed that, since the badger spends its day in the underground dark and is largely active at night, its reliance upon scent and hearing rather than sight is appropriate and that the strength of vision might gradually be much reduced as generations pass. However, it may be too, that although the badger has become nocturnal in habit, since its eyes have remained more suited to diurnal existence, it is possible that a return to greater daytime activity could enhance its reliance upon and use of its eyes.

There are occasions when I suspect that the senses, including sight, are kept at a more tensely alert level. When cubs are small the female appears particularly vigilant. Her conduct seems to suggest that eyes are watchful of security, but even then sound or smell seem to be required to confirm whatever unaccustomed stimuli are received by the eyes. The eye may command alertness but ears or nose decide action.

One reason advanced to support the theory that the badger is almost blind is that sometimes a small mammal scurries quite close without the badger appearing to take very much notice. In addition, it is said that badgers pay remarkably little attention to dim torchlight. This is open to question. If the person with the torch is a frequent visitor to an undisturbed and unattacked sett there is often great tolerance of his presence. In normal circumstances a badger will return into the sett if there is a white light but not if quite dim light is masked by a suitable red filter.

In notes based on watching at a Charnwood sett T. J. Whall[31] expressed the opinion that 'the badger's vision is limited to a few inches from its nose'. He said that a badger picked up small morsels of food with the mouth open only a little way and that if a large item of food was offered the mouth only opened wide enough at the last moment.

This may be so, but the position of the badger's nose and mouth are such that often the nose is likely to touch food before the mouth. This is particularly disadvantageous where liquid is concerned and an adult badger may well have developed an approach to food which makes a very restricted mouth opening habitual until it is clear that this is impracticable. Normally the badger's food is relatively small in size so habit may be established.

Whilst one cannot dismiss the observations of experienced naturalists it is fair to say that not all watchers share the view that the badger is almost blind. A colleague told me of one of his local badger's activity in his garden climbing upon and jumping off a quite tall compost heap. I too have watched a badger climb a few feet and I know that some climb to collect fruit which also suggests some capacity of vision. Vigorous play is of such a character that vision seems to be used to a considerable extent. Certainly, when cubs are small the sow is particularly vigilant and it seems to me that her conduct suggests seeing and looking as well as scenting and listening.

During 1973 I was able to watch badgers only very rarely. My spare time, nowadays most limited, was then particularly restricted partly because of the extra time taken by my involvement in Parliamentary activity connected with the Badgers Act. However, I did sit one evening upon a tree trunk by a sett. My back was towards another tree so there was no break in the badgers' accustomed visual pattern. What little wind there was blew upon my face. Two cubs and an adult appeared, the adult first, the two cubs immediately behind and quick to commence play before they were really out of the entrance.

Play was boisterous for a few minutes whilst the adult scratched. When I took a flash photograph there was a brief, almost imperceptible pause, in the cubs' play and in the boar's grooming. Then there came the noise of the film being moved, not loud, but quite audible to the badgers only ten or twelve feet away. This caused a slightly longer pause in the play and scratching. After another couple of minutes I took a second photograph. This time more notice was taken for the pause was longer and the subsequent camera noise caused all three badgers to move warily and stand close to the sett entrance. However, after perhaps twenty or thirty seconds play resumed.

Two or three minutes later the two cubs romped very close towards me and I took another photograph. The adult then took a more attentive attitude and the cubs appeared to see me and shrank back upon the ground. I moved the film along and, as before, the adult turned facing me. Then, spontaneously, all three animals scurried into the sett.

I consider that the badgers did see me if only vaguely. Visual experience then, may have to be confirmed by another sense before action is taken. This does not mean that there is such limited visual capacity as some observers believe. In any case a badger's sight seems more efficient than my photography!

I believe it is also true that at the sett escape or defence action are not invariably stimulated by noise. Occasionally sudden and strange noise seems to be little regarded, but scent always receives a swifter response. One trace of a suspicious odour when the animal wishes to leave the sett and the delay in emergence may be extensive. From this it can be deduced that scent is the most dominant of the badger's senses.

The sow often seems more suspicious and warier than the boar. I am doubtful, though, whether this extra alertness of the female badger is fully maintained throughout the year and significantly the sow is particularly vigilant when there are cubs in or near the sett. One June evening some years ago I walked slowly behind a sow for three or four hundred yards. At first I kept ten or a dozen yards behind her but gradually I moved nearer until I was not more than seven or eight feet away. Occasionally she stopped, three times she turned round but without alarm or anger. She was quite a young animal, probably in her second summer. There were no cubs at her sett that year.

The following year there were three cubs at the sett. I cannot be absolutely certain that the sow which I had followed and seen on occasions during subsequent months was the mother of these cubs. I think she was, but her behaviour and attitudes were different. The relaxed and tolerant attitude encountered along the ride the year before had gone. At the slightest sign the cubs were swiftly returned to the sett and re-emergence was quite long-delayed and hesitant. Once or twice my wait was much extended by this sow's most wary conduct. Before the cubs emerged she savoured and assessed the air for very long periods.

Emergence is usually preceded by this cautious testing of the air from within the entrance. Often several minutes may elapse before there is confidence that all is well and sometimes one can almost watch this calculation of security. Of course, where there has been persecution the preliminaries are extremely careful indeed. Where there has been no disturbance in living memory the decision to emerge may be very quickly taken.

Once satisfied of safety the adult emerges and is likely to begin its toilet. The first action may be to balance upon three legs whilst one hind foot vigorously scratches with a concentrated energy. Often, though, the grooming, the attention to irritated areas, is carried out by pressing and rubbing against a scratching post. Often a nearby tree is selected for this purpose and used by generations of badgers so that at appropriate heights it is worn smooth. In some areas a large rock or stone may be used instead of a tree.

The cubs' first above-ground activity each evening is usually recreation rather than grooming, and they play with an abounding and delightful enthusiasm. Some of the play is quite fascinating, rather similar to that of puppies but perhaps a little more imaginative. Several times I watched two families of cubs, five altogether, all of similar size, spending a great deal of time somersaulting down a steep slope into their large sett. The five appeared to queue and take turns to roll head over heels down the eight or nine feet of the slope which I could see. Usually they came up from another entrance a few yards away but sometimes there was a collision as one eager cub tried to climb up the slope while another one rolled down. Then the chattering of playing cubs turned into a little squall of fleeting, if immature, rage.

As the summer passes play becomes more boisterous; mock fights are rather rough. There are more moments when group activity is broken as individual cubs stop to examine a particular object. However, whilst play may become a little more sporadic there are occasions when the adults join in the tussling. There is generally a direct sexual significance in the play of adult badgers for it frequently precedes mating.

It is difficult to comment with precision on the origins of the badger's patterns of behaviour. Clearly cubs' play is instinctive and largely related to essential future activity. Much of it is such that combative skill is developed, but the identification and measurement of objects and the recognition of food items are also learned. I once scattered chocolate drops around a sett so that the evening play was then interrupted by the snapping-up of titbits and by the momentary and voiced rivalries which resulted.

The cubs make a squealing chattering or chuckling sort of noise which does not carry far. Nor are the normal noises of the adult at all loud. The main sound made is a low, soft, almost purring growl. Dr Neal noticed that the boar made this sound at the sett entrance before the rest of the family emerged. I have heard this noise myself when the boar has appeared and it seemed to suggest a call to the sow, although sometimes the boar moved away before the sow had time to respond. The adult badger will also snarl and, in peaceful mood, often repeat the chattering noise more usually made by cubs.

Badgers can produce a yell, an ear-piercing noise which has been heard infrequently. As yet there is no firm explanation for it. Some have suggested that it is a mating call, others that it is the mourning cry of a bereaved mate. It is not only a mating call since it has been heard outside the appropriate periods. Similarly it has been heard when there is no evidence of a badger death, but it could be a keening call nevertheless. I have only heard this noise on one occasion and then there seemed to be no immediate reason for it.

I believe it to be a call of loneliness, possibly uttered by independent young and unpaired animals—and quite young badgers have been said to have made this strident sound. If the badger was not nocturnal in habit we might not have to seek the explanation in the dark. However, I have seen no evidence that this yell is a response to a full moon!

Of course, during the short nights of midsummer, badgers are likely to emerge before dark. I believe that if they are undisturbed or unmolested they are then, especially, likely to be above ground rather earlier and more often than is assumed. Again, this is hard to prove beyond doubt but all badger observers will have some experience of early emergence. It is rare though that the emergent badger strays far from the sett during the day.

One early evening, in good light, four or five years ago when some young people were walking towards me in a local wood, a badger went slowly across the path in front of them. They were delighted—as I was when, as soon as they walked on, the badger came back along a path having cut the corner of the rides' crossing. He ambled along, unhurriedly, but with the fairly quick-footed rolling gait customary in the unworried animal.

Pauses in a badger's progress are frequent. In part this may be a safety device to permit listening for security but this is not the only explanation. The pauses are taken also to allow the proprietorial or identificative 'musking' which is common amongst members of this family and many other carnivores. Musking is mainly a territorial marking activity but, since the badger relies upon its nose so much, it also allows it to develop greater familiarity with, and activity within, its territory.

Of course, pauses also allow an opportunity to detect intrusion. Arthur Killingley, the Mammal Society's Badger Survey compiler, has described[14] a young badger's foraging, which was closely watched by a companion and himself. They were largely ignored, but another badger 50yd away was listened to most attentively. Mr Killingley's walk allowed him to observe the animal feed and he also noted that the cub musked on one occasion. With an adult, particularly a boar, he would almost certainly have observed more frequent musking.

Badgers are not the only mammals which leave scent marking. So do the fox, the wolf, and many other predators. In most cases the marking is achieved by the use of a tiny secretion of fluid from the scent glands which lie under the root of the tail. This is so with the badger. The fluid secreted may be used for other purposes than the marking of territory, as with the skunk, but badgers do not commonly secrete this fluid for other purposes. Sometimes a more voluminous discharge occurs. This probably happens as much from excitement as from terror, possibly but not invariably at the time of mating. A fearful encounter may also cause the larger emission, and a more powerful odour has been detected when occupancy of a sett has just commenced.

Normally though, scent emission is minute, and the smell created by the badger cannot be said to be in any way either offensive or malodorous. I suppose if the sensibility of the urban human nose declined much more then the smell of a badger would be entirely undetectable instead of largely so. *Meles meles* does not offend our British nostrils, which is lucky for those of us who like to watch badgers at close quarters!

The fact that natural enemies are scarce may have caused an unaggressive scent capacity to evolve. Whatever the reason we are able with wit, and after calculation, to watch a wild animal at close quarters without harm, danger or serious offence.

CHAPTER 3

THE BADGER'S YEAR

WINTER

Until recent years it was supposed that the badger hibernated for long periods during the winter months. Some naturalists held the view that the badger, whilst not so soundly in suspension as the hedgehog, was nevertheless hibernant. In fact the British badger does not hibernate.

No one could claim that in harsh weather the badger does not stay in its sett for periods of over twenty-four hours and there are records of badgers remaining below ground for a very long time. In one case a badger was left to choose whether to stay in its sett or leave to face a trap and it did not emerge until a couple of weeks had elapsed when it was in an emaciated condition. The normal circumstances faced by our wild badgers are such that choices and persistent pressures of this kind are fortunately not general and, in winter months particularly, human interference at a level so vicious as the example referred to is unlikely.

In undisturbed areas I believe the badger does emerge from its sett every night. If the weather is really severe I would expect that on some nights it might only visit a nearby dung-pit, possibly scratch, and then return below. I think it unlikely that this restricted activity would be repeated on the following night and that it would be even more unlikely for a third night of toilet-only emergence to occur.

I cannot claim to have spent many frozen hours or nights confirming this view. However, I have visited setts in winter as have many other naturalists and experience shows that badgers do leave occupied setts during cold periods. It is not necessary to spend all night by a sett to provide evidence for this belief. Indeed, the possible extra inducement to remain below ground may come from the suspicions which a watcher's presence possibly arouse. Daytime visits to setts should confirm the view that there is activity in winter. The most obvious signs of this are tracks in snow or mud—and the badger's track is recognisable—maintained use of paths, the movement of bedding can be seen at sett entrances, the use of dung-pits and traces of fresh digging.

Evidence is also available from those who actually catch sight of badgers in winter. People who live near to setts and put out food for badgers note that food is taken at all times, winter included. Then there is the evidence which comes from hunting activity in winter. An earth-stopper will block setts during the evening before the hunt in order to prevent the fox from going to ground. This interference may well keep badgers below ground that night. However, emergence from the sett is almost certain on the second night. It is little use a sett or earth being stopped two or three nights before a hunt and the opening up of a sett on the same night only a few hours after stopping is by no means unknown.

It is clear, therefore, that the badger does not sleep away the winter. If it did then its physical condition in March would be rather less robust than it appears to be. Although a mature adult will weigh three or four pounds more at the beginning of a severe winter than in March, if it drew its sustenance entirely from its own reserves as it would in hibernation, the loss of condition would be much more marked. This moderate weight loss is an effect of the reduced availability and variety of food rather than of any failure to eat.

In Britain, however, the badger may sleep soundly for more of its time during winter particularly in harsh weather when it might be reluctant to move more than a short distance from its chamber. These tendencies may be more marked in the least hospitable areas where badgers may spend longer periods in their setts. This suggests that thousands of years ago in colder times badgers may once have been a partially hibernating species. It clearly isn't now, even though there is some evidence, if not entirely conclusive evidence, that foreign badgers do sleep for long periods in colder winters than those we experience in Britain.

It is difficult to estimate the amount of time which a badger spends above ground at any period of the year. However, I do not agree with the estimates offered in the 1920s that the animal spends one hour above for every seventy hours below ground in winter. I would not disagree with an estimate of one-quarter of the time above ground, though so much depends upon the severity of the winter or the nature of the locality itself and some time may well be spent remarkably close to the surface near the sett entrance.

In some areas the decay of vegetation may mean that the sett is much more open to view and more easily visited at this time of the year. This might lead to considerable disturbance. In such a case winter hours spent above ground may be much less than those spent by badgers at a sett in a more isolated and undisturbed area when, even during a cold January, one-third of the time may be spent above ground and considerable distances could be covered taking the animal quite far from the sett.

Of course, winter brings its problems. In really cold weather digging may be extremely difficult, even for the strongest badger. Consequently, there may be drastic changes in diet so that a larger proportion of the food consumed is likely to be of vegetable matter. In frozen conditions most of the badger's food has undoubtedly to be obtained without digging and this could mean a temporary inadequacy of quantity and nourishment, severe perhaps in exceptionally harsh periods when scavenging may be occasionally rewarded. But normal winters do not present real problems for most badgers. The animal's coat is appropriate; its stiff texture assists the withstanding of hard weather and, possibly, the badger's quite thick skin is also an assistance.

Like other animals the badger relishes comfort. Tame badgers, for instance, often like to lie very close to the domestic fire. This does not mean that they are likely to perish when exercising in the outside cold. I have owned Samoyed dogs for almost twenty years and they exhibit the same tendency. Storm, my present dog, great-great-grandson of our first Samoyed, will spend half the evening, from choice, lying on cold concrete. However, if he is indoors he will lie so close to the fire that he has, on occasion, singed his coat. Yet these dogs are recent descendants of animals which came to Britain after Arctic or Antarctic expeditions and, before then, hundreds of generations lived through Siberian winters. They have the type of coat and other physical attributes, large furred feet, bushy tails, thick ears, which assist such survival and make British winters little of a challenge to them. So it is with our badgers, for the species can be found in parts of the world where conditions during the winter months are much more extreme than our own, yet a fondness for warmth is marked and in cold weather several badgers may sleep crowded together to ensure that rest is within a warm and cosy chamber.

After the middle of winter the cubs are born. We cannot be at all precise about the actual date of birth as cubs have been known to be born as early as January or as late as April. It is probably correct to say that most cubs are born before the end of February, perhaps a little earlier in the south than in the north. If I had to state a mean date I would select 20 February but this can only be a guess. In my own northern locality I would expect birth to be a couple of days after this and even a week later in the north of Scotland.

Cubs are born below ground in a large nest within a specially occupied breeding chamber. At birth they have soft, short and pale-coloured coats with little or no hair on the underparts. They are blind and remain so for upwards of a fortnight. Weight is not easily ascertainable, of course, but it is likely that they are relatively tiny, not more than 7 or 8oz (200g) in weight. If one compares the weight of a cub with that of a puppy of a breed of dog which is of similar weight and size to the badger it may well be that the badger whelp is a little smaller.

Mortimer Batten assumed[2] that there were far more males than females and suggested that one major cause of this was that sows were likely to die after parturition. Obviously some mortality occurs but, considering the anatomy of the species and the size of the cubs, this does not seem to me to be a particular hazard facing this animal.

Just as knowledge of the size of cubs and of their date of birth is inevitably imprecise so is it also difficult to state the size of any litter. Certainly large litters are unusual and quite often only one cub is born—or survives. Litters of four or five are not uncommon but two or three cubs are more likely. As I mentioned earlier I have seen five cubs playing together at one very large sett but they were from two litters. It is likely that six or more cubs seen together are from two litters rather than one. That two litters are similar in size merely means that both were born more or less at the same time.

During the winter months bedding changes continue but this is generally a much more marked activity after the cubs are born. Indeed, increased bed-changing in late winter can be circumstantial evidence of birth.

In the early days of life the cubs are extremely vulnerable. If the sett is seriously attacked at this time there is a real possibility that the sow will devour very young cubs. Other species have been known to eat their young and this has been ascribed either to a dietary inadequacy or to a fear-reaction. Normally, once the early days are over the sow is unlikely to do this for she is rightly regarded as a devoted dam. Batten writes[2] that on one occasion a sow was carrying a cub in her mouth when she was attacked by dogs. She kept moving, bearing the dogs' biting without retaliation, holding her cub so that although she was injured both escaped.

If a mature pair are living in a sett cubs are likely to have been born there. If there are no cubs it may be that either a litter was born but failed to survive, that the sow had not reached breeding age or had not conceived.

Just as evidence of birth can be surmised from the increased incidence of bed-changing so it can be from the fact that the parents of a litter are likely to mate again shortly after cubs are born. This led to the belief that badgers had a gestation period of one year's duration. We now know that this is improbable but the fact remains that after cubs are born and this is almost always before winter can be regarded as finally ended, the adult pair re-mate.

It is likely that as soon as the sow is in breeding condition, the actual mating will be with the existing mate or the boar currently in dominant position in the family hierarchy, or both. This is likely to occur in the summer when the sow is young. An older sow can, of course, be presumed to receive the boar shortly after cubs are born but this period of mating is not the only one, for mating appears to be repeated at intervals until the autumn.

SPRING

This season sees the cubs emerge and begin their play which becomes more boisterous as each evening passes. It is generally assumed that the cubs do not emerge until they are at least seven or eight weeks old. I have been told of one incident, very early in the year, which may well have been a first emergence when the sow came out of the sett extremely slowly shepherding before her the tiniest cub my informants had ever seen, which seemed overawed by the new dimension of its existence. Such hesitant docility soon passes, certainly before May is out the cubs' desire to play is almost irrepressible; so much so that they appear to enjoy the first half-hour after emergence most of all.

I now believe that individual emergences during daylight hours are not at all unusual either for adults or cubs in spring and summer. One late April afternoon, at about 3 pm I stood within two or three feet of a cub which slowly wandered out of the sett to stay for a while upon the ridge of earth thrown from below. It remained above ground for about fifteen minutes.

At the same sett I caught a glimpse of a cub during one spring afternoon the following year. On several occasions I have noticed other evidence of day-time emergence. Perhaps when cubs like the ones I have seen leave their chamber the rest of the family has been sleeping. Possibly the wakeful cub could not gainsay either curiosity or energy. Whatever the reason, I believe that both young and old badgers will leave their sleeping chamber during the day from time to time. Much depends, of course, upon the locality and security of the sett.

I have visited one sett during several afternoons in the last seven or eight years. On a number of occasions I have heard them return below as I approached the sett and I have seen evidence of very fresh digging. I have also noticed a circle of open ground about a yard in diameter which I suspect was a day-bed.

As spring passes the cubs are weaned and become more active. By summer they can forage in their own right but during April and May they are still very much under instruction. Like other predators they learn from the imitation of adults and through play. Much is learned through activity but all the time experience through the senses is acquired. So the cubs learn the family territory and become accustomed to using the paths or tracks which may have been used for many generations. During play they develop the skills which life will demand and increase their capacity to recognise objects and, therefore, to survive within their particular environment.

Soon after first emergence the cubs begin to use the dung-pits. Whilst cubs are small any soiled bedding is regularly changed, further evidence that the badger is a particularly fastidious creature. By the end of their second month some cubs appear to have learned the habits essential to the species. 'House-training' is usually completed by the end of April. This characteristic seems to be of an instinctive nature. Cubs taken into domesticity appear to be naturally clean at a very early age. A young sow badger reared in a home in my constituency was certainly a very clean animal. She insisted that her bedding should be clean and regularly refused to sleep on a blanket unless it was washed very frequently. At a very early age 'accidents' ceased. From this point of view it may appear that adaptation to domestication is easy, but there are other disadvantages, not the least being the species' tremendously inquisitive character. This, like the clean habits, is also noticeable in the wild.

In early May it would be extremely unusual to see any sign of obviously fouled bedding taken from the sett. Of course, it is not possible to be precise about the age of the cubs when day-time continence is complete, partly because one normally cannot be exactly sure of the actual date of birth. However, it is a fair conclusion that the age of complete cleanliness is reached not later than during the third month.

With the lengthening days and the improving weather of spring the diet available to the badger is more varied and abundant. The satisfaction of hunger becomes less of a problem and the time required to obtain adequate food is likely to be much reduced. This allows both greater selection of diet and longer periods of play to be possible.

Often, the boar will not remain at the sett for a long period. He may join in the family's summer play but such activity frequently seems to develop sexual excitement. Otherwise he may leave the sett alone and begin solitary foraging, although frequently the family move off together.

There is obviously some comfort and content in mutual contact within the particular family, and even a badger which appears to be engaged in solitary activity visits the setts of its kin during its nightly foraging. A large number of the established paths in any area actually lead from one sett to another. Sometimes a visiting badger will enter other setts within the family territory; at other times it may merely stand at the entrance before moving on. However, whether the sett is entered or not the visit will be marked by musking to leave an identifiable trace. Much may depend upon the occupants of a visited sett. Where it contains young cubs, then entrance by another badger is unlikely. Where, late in the year, the occupant is a sow which is in mating condition one may well find one or two males nearby or entering the sett. Indeed, Batten's references to wandering male badgers may really be an example of boars from one area visiting a locality where there is a female on 'heat'.

Whilst autumn is regarded as the major period of bedding collection, at this time of the year extensive if sporadic activity can be noted. I have seen a badger bringing bedding out of the sett on three occasions. A good deal of effort is involved in the movement of material. Both fore feet are used for balance and to keep the bundled material together as the badger moves from or into the sett—backwards. I once stood close by a sett watching an emergence with bedding in spring. A considerable amount of noise was involved as a large quantity of material was removed. The process took quite a long time as activity from the first sound to actual emergence with bedding occupied nearly fifteen minutes.

Bedding activity inevitably occupies a good deal of time. Considering this, and the tendency to sociability and play, it seems clear that the badger does not normally have to spend the great bulk of its wakeful or surface hours in pursuit of food, unless wintry conditions are particularly severe, but it is doubtful whether this theory could be comprehensively applied to all British badgers, including those living in the more barren areas.

SUMMER

Often a couple of pairs and their cubs live in one large sett although each litter is born in separate chambers. In most localities though, a number of setts are occupied by units of the same family and it may be that cubs are reared in different but closely neighbouring setts. By early summer there is inevitably a great deal of contact between the families. It is not at all unusual, particularly if there has been a lot of interference or, if one of the parents has died or been killed, for a family of cubs to move at quite an early age, perhaps to combine with another litter.

By early July, if an earlier move has not taken place, the breeding chamber or sett is likely to be vacated and the different pairs or survivors of pairs and their cubs gather together. The sett or chamber chosen for joint occupancy is likely to be the most secure and the longest established in the territory. However, even during this period, movement between setts and temporary occupancy of other setts by small groups and by individuals is not uncommon.

If and when a whole family congregates it does not mean that there will be a really massive gathering even where successful breeding occurs, for litters are small and the casualty rate quite severe. If there is an imbalance between the sexes some of the young ones may tend to move away, so ensuring that in any locality numbers are relatively stable. However, any movement to another area would be likely to bring serious danger to the individual emigrant from other and unrelated badgers.

This means that family or clan numbers tend to be quite small. The largest number I have known to congregate at one sett is eleven. No doubt there may be occasional groups which may reach into the teens in size but I would consider any late summer gathering of over ten to be above average at this time. At the largest sett in my area, perhaps the largest sett in South Yorkshire, the highest number observed in recent years has been twelve. This included the cubs of at least two litters, one of which had been reared at that sett, the other at one a little distance away. The largest gathering of badgers noted in South Yorkshire was one of sixteen observed by J. S. Griffith some years ago. From my own recent experience of the same sett I doubt if there are many more than half that number present now.

I assume that any gathering of badgers involves only a move from one part of a territory to another. This seems to explain most congregations for they appear to occur when the family collects after midsummer. Then cubs are brought together and a more congretated pattern of living develops for a while. It has been said that badger setts are happy colonies and that relationships are cordial within the family. Of course, for various reasons, mainly mating rivalries, tiffs and shifts in living patterns do occur.

By the end of summer the close bonds of the adult pair and their cubs of the year begin to loosen with the departure of the paired animals from the chamber in which the cubs were bred. By this time the younger adults, unmated the previous year, will be sufficiently mature to breed. Generally the surviving adults confirm their previous pairing relationship. However, whilst the same pairs may appear to remain together, it is always possible that a sow may be mated by more than one boar, an occurrence that I have evidence of. Nevertheless pairing usually appears to be upon a lifetime basis, although mortality rates suggest that the lifetimes involved are not lengthy.

As stated previously, the first mating of the new season occurs soon after the cubs are born. The sow is then in breeding condition for at least two further periods during the year. Before mating there is usually considerable play. Often, in summer months the play involves the whole family before the boar commences mating activity. This can take rather a long time. The boar mounts and may seize the sow's neck or ears in his teeth although no serious injury is likely to be inflicted. Any other badgers in the vicinity are likely to be warned off. The strongest and dominant boar in any locality may mate with all or most of the sows in addition to the mating with their usual partner.

When the mating periods are over the family congregation may tend to break up with its component pairs beginning their more separate existence. The as yet unattached young usually remain within the family group although there may well be some movement into other territory.

During the summer months food supplies are generally very abundant and, whilst the nights are shorter so that the duration of foraging is more restricted, it is unlikely that any normally healthy animal will find difficulty in obtaining sufficient food. During these months in fact the badger may ignore many opportunities to eat for, to a real extent, it may be able to indulge its particular choice of food.

Fortunately the badger has a tough skin so that attacks upon the nests of wasp and bee are tolerable and a sweet tooth can be satisfied. I suppose that such a meal must rank as a high peak of summer activity for any badger, as a cause of real delight, for clearly honey is regarded as very desirable. Of course, it is not really likely that such meals are terribly frequent, although it is certain that the intake of animal protein is greater at this time, the peak of nature's fecundity.

During these months the badger consumes many small creatures the variety of which is likely to depend upon population cycles. When a prey species falls in number badgers do not move on to other areas, they merely turn to the other food items which may not have been eaten during the glut of another species.

So summer passes, the time of comfort and food choice. As growth continues so there may be greater security, too. Thick vegetation may hide the sett and discourage visitors.

AUTUMN

Until recently it was suspected that sows tended to produce

young only in alternate years. This is not the case but the reason for such a belief is not hard to seek. A female will appear adult in her second spring but she will not have produced cubs. In the following year it is likely that a litter will be produced. Thus it might be thought that alternate years of breeding are likely for, obviously, in many localities the proportion of sows which are under three years of age may be extremely high. In the first autumn of a sow's life she will not be pregnant but in the following year pregnancy is probable, and thereafter an annual pregnancy is likely. Given a relatively low life-expectancy it may be that only a small minority of female badgers will produce more than one or two litters.

With the start of autumn the year's cubs have become rather more independent. At this time new diggings can be found and new setts are dug or old ones reopened. Often these are merely the practisings of cubs and since the badger population is unlikely to explode, numerous extra setts are quite unnecessary. At this time of year a family of five or six badgers may open up and occupy, at least temporarily, a similar number of setts.

Now the mated pairs prepare to occupy their selected breeding quarters. The mature sow is likely to be pregnant and the previous cubs usually—not invariably—assume some independence of occupation. They do not normally maintain the same degree of very close-knit life and they may not now share the same sett or the same area of large single setts as their parents. Often they may wander quite a distance away and enter the territory of unrelated badgers where they risk severe mauling. There is at least the possibility that they will establish new setts or reoccupy inactive setts from which the previous family have disappeared or been destroyed. In some areas badgers may have been wiped out at a particularly attractive sett on several occasions. This re-occupation will be due either to other members of the same family clinging to a sett with persistent determination or to a spill-over from neighbouring areas taking place. Mr A. Bloomfield in *The Field* posed an interesting question, with regard to re-occupation. How does the badger know which holes to work at when taking over a disused sett? My own view is that any re-occupation which takes place is likely to be based upon the memory of earlier visits. A sett may be unoccupied for two or three years but one or two badgers in the area may be several years older than that and visits to the sett will have been made during its previous occupancy and on various occasions, if not to inspect the interior at least around the area of the sett, during the period of disuse. We should remember that whilst badgers may not always roam over a wide area they are not to be expected to confine themselves to activity within a short radius of their setts. Movement outside the family territory arouses hostility from any badgers in possession, for territorial consciousness is very marked, although relationships within a sett are normally unstrained.

By the end of autumn when the breeding quarters are occupied by the mature pairs the greatest amount of bedding collection can be observed. There are still periods of partial congregation, especially during cold periods, and visiting between setts is always frequent.

The reproductive arrangements of the badger are unique. If mating leading to pregnancy occurs in July and the cubs are born in the following February this means that the badger's gestation is seven months in duration. Indeed, since in the past it was thought that the mating leading to conception was that which followed the birth of cubs, a gestation of about twelve months' length was accepted. We now know that this is rather unlikely, although it is by no means certain that only a summer mating is fertile. Perhaps mating at any time might lead to conception. However, a summer mating may be more likely to lead to breeding since the shorter period of gestation provides less opportunity for abortion or miscarriage to occur.

In most species the course of pregnancy is one of steady development. Badgers could be expected to produce cubs after a pregnancy of little more than eight or nine weeks since a bitch will whelp on or about the sixty-third day after mating. However, the pregnancy of the badger seems likely to take at least three months longer than that of other mammals of similar anatomical character and physical complexity and size.

The lengthy duration of pregnancy is not due to an excessively slow but steady embryonic development. In normal mammals the fertilised egg, the blastocyst, swiftly attaches itself to the lining of the womb in the process known as implantation. In the case of the badger after the blastocyst is formed there is a great delay in implantation in the embryo attaching itself to the uterus. Pregnancy then appears to include a state of suspension. This delay in implantation may last four months or more.

It has been noted that in mid-January, embryos of cubs were less than 10mm long whilst Dr Neal[19] noted that one embryo examined on 3 February was 100mm in length. Thus, it can be suggested that implantation is unlikely to occur much before the new year and that from then the development of the embryo takes place at a more normal or rapid rate. Of course, the badger is not the only mammal in which this delay in implantation occurs, the roe deer, for example, reveals the same phenomenon.

It may be that the relatively small numbers of cubs in litters produced by the badger is a result of the long gestation during which, for various reasons, the future litter size could be reduced.

So the cycle of the badger's year is experienced; birth in late winter, then mating again and the preparation for a new family and the growth of the independence of the young badgers during the autumn.

During the year digging and cleaning activity continues each in its own sporadic if frequent pattern. As months pass so the balance of diet shifts in response to the change in seasons and the varied opportunities presented by the diversities of the year.

The head of a family is generally a boar and there can be some rivalry for dominance. However, even though a male may appear to hold and to exert authority it seems clear that the sow assumes prime responsibility for the cubs. I doubt if the boar is allowed much underground contact with them, certainly not during their early days of life although by the end of spring he seems to be regarded quite amicably.

Autumn ends with the occupation of freshly lined and possibly newly extended or re-opened sleeping chambers. These at this time should be occupied by well-fed creatures amply prepared to face winter and the next year.

It is very difficult to say exactly when a badger will leave the sett. As a general rule I would say that emergence occurs between fifteen and forty-five minutes after sunset. The season's changes are reflected in the patterns and times of emergence, nearer to sunset in summer later in winter, but it is impossible to be precise. Badgers in an undisturbed area may well be abroad earlier; those living closest to man may commence the night's activity rather late. Winter months apart, when I visit a sett I usually plan to arrive about fifteen or twenty minutes after sunset. Sometimes I have observed badgers already out and about when I have arrived, although quite often the wait for emergence has been longer than theory might anticipate.

Hard and fast rules cannot be laid down but perhaps the following estimates will serve as a very rough guide to the time of emergence as at Greenwich Mean Time.

January	6.30 pm	July	8.30 pm
February	6.30 pm	August	8.00 pm
March	7.00 pm	September	7.30 pm
April	7.30 pm	October	7.00 pm
May	8.00 pm	November	6.30 pm
June	8.30 pm	December	6.00 pm

CHAPTER 4

SUBSISTENCE AND HEALTH

The badger's teeth and jaws show clearly that it is a carnivore: the large, deeply rooted canines and the structure and joint of the jaw reveal that it could scarcely be a grazing animal. However, the molars are large so that whilst grazing is not really natural, a wide range of foods can nevertheless be bitten, torn and crushed if not chewed. The badger then, whilst essentially a flesh-eater, can and does consume a very varied diet. Mortimer Batten's comment that a badger could eat anything short of corrugated iron was not at all inappropriate.[2] Yet there are staple foods and badgers could not long survive without a considerable intake of animal protein and other nutrients not directly available from vegetable matter so, although considerable quantities of the latter are consumed, it does not represent anything like the total food intake.

Very little is known about the cubs' pattern of feeding. Clearly they depend upon lactation for many weeks. I have watched cubs between two and four months of age leave the sett on a number of occasions. Invariably they have played with and near the sow, showing no apparent interest in feeding from her, an unnatural inclination if they had not fed either recently or at least during the preceding few hours spent in the sett.

Since it is extremely unusual for badgers to carry food into the sett this suggests that the cubs are sustained on milk for quite a considerable time. I believe that there is another tenable explanation—that badgers begin weaning by consuming food regurgitated by the parents. This would not be at all astonishing for regurgitation, particularly by the dam, is normal in many carnivorous species. Many good brood bitches instinctively regurgitate which suggests that the habit is innate. Given the badger's pattern of life, if regurgitation is not practised then the feeding of cubs must be such as to make the species even more unusual than it is already known to be. Cubs grow quite rapidly and it would be surprising if such growth was entirely maintained from lactation only.

Even quite long lactation does not give cause to dispel the regurgitation theory since this would provide a most suitable method of weaning for this species and regurgitative practice would fit in with the badger's way of life. Usually the boar, which is unlikely to be occupying the same chamber as the sow in the first stages of the cubs' life, leaves the sett first. He may do so without waking others although this seems to be highly unlikely. A certain amount of noise is made underground before and during emergence. If the cubs are awake, part of the time which elapses between the boar's first movements and the cubs' emergence could very naturally be occupied in feeding activity. If cubs are *not* fed then the prime interest in play on emergence is surprising. An earlier satisfaction of hunger seems likely although an evening feed may be less likely to be from regurgitation than a meal taken earlier in the day.

Only conjecture can be offered to support this theory. Soiled bedding could be analysed to ascertain if there is evidence of the remains of partially digested food. Perhaps extensive research into cubs' feeding habits may be undertaken one day. Until then we can only guess. Our certain knowledge is that cubs are fed below ground for many weeks.

D

The demands made by the food requirement of cubs may be more easily sustained since litters are usually small. Physiologically the species should be able to cope with litters of six or more. The fact that there may well be only three cubs or less means that demands upon the sow are less than severe.

During their play cubs—and adults—will seize upon such edible morsels as they may encounter, whilst cubs will sometimes use scraps of edible matter as play objects before consumption. From time to time I have put food down for wild badgers. At one sett I have scattered a wide variety of foodstuffs. Almost everything has been accepted including dog biscuits and household scraps but the most favoured contributions were bread and honey and chocolate drops.

It is beyond all doubt that badgers do have a great fondness for sweet things. Richard Jefferies believed that the badger dug up the wasps' nests for the larvae, not for honey which the wasp does not secrete: 'It is the nest of the bumble-bee which the badger roots up for the honey . . . It is very sweet like that of the Give-bee but a little darker in colour and much less in quantity.'[12]

A wild bee's nest is approached with eagerness and determination and invariably the badger presses home its ravaging for it desires honey greatly. The defence of wasps and bees may be largely ineffective because of the badger's tough skin and harsh protecting coat: in the past badger skin has been used for articles which were required to be durable like pistol holsters.

I once placed a trail of chocolate drops along a badger path leading from the sett for about 50yd and then along a ride for a similar distance. The trail was laid on one early July evening at 8.00 pm. I looked again a little later and saw no sign of any chocolate although I did see a badger on the path. This entirely circumstantial evidence suggests the possibility that a badger could be conditioned by food rewards in certain conditions.

Others have provided food and confectionery for badgers with interesting results. Neil Clark who has visited one North

Yorkshire sett with unfailing regularity for several years usually scatters Sugar Puffs. Dr Paget, who once accompanied Mr Clark, told me that not only did it seem as if the animal expected the provision but also that it was quite unworried by the close presence of his companion. One boar badger, in fact, on leaving the sett clearly picked up the stranger's scent and returned to the hole it left, only to reappear from another entrance a few moments later. At this point it was closer to the familiar scent and left the sett immediately to begin eating the breakfast cereal. Even camera noises did not cause the boar to lift its head, which was only achieved when Mr Clark who was only a few feet from the animal shouted 'Hoy!' quite forcefully. The animal responded with a brief, disinterested lift of its head before feeding was resumed. I am grateful for the photograph on page 107 taken by Mr Clark at this sett.

A couple of years before I entered Parliament I made a lot of visits to one South Yorkshire sett over a period of several weeks and many times scattered food nearby. Five cubs were then playing around the sett. On one warm evening I left my coat at the edge of the sett under an elder and moved nearer to the hole from which the badgers usually emerged. Watching the cubs play I heard a slight sound behind me and saw one cub nosing my coat with interest, its head in the pocket which contained the bag of delicacies for the night. My quick movement startled the cub which disappeared down the nearest entrance. The other cubs and the sow also descended. However, they reappeared after only a few minutes to discover and eat the food which I had scattered about after their fright. A degree of familiarity had obviously developed for otherwise the inevitable taint would have made the food immediately unacceptable.

The tempting of badger palates is not a particularly modern development. *Gentleman's Recreation* advises 'take but a piece of Pork and train it over a badger's Burrow if he be within you shall quickly see him appear'.[5] I tried this without any pleasantly astonishing result. The pork was taken but not during my observation.

One Sunday newspaper in September 1973 carried a photo story of a badger in Wales which regularly visited a pub and was given a drink of beer. If the badger was quite wild it was clearly a most untypical animal, perhaps more astonishing for its visits to a pub than for its consumption of strong drink which may have a considerable sugar content.

Of course, the vast majority of badgers are not fed by man and in normal times it is not desirable for them to be fed artificially. Reliance upon man as a food provider is not to be encouraged in the best interest of any wild species, especially in an urban situation, as shown by the scavenging foxes of suburbia.

The badger's natural food obviously varies according to the season. In later months, particularly during the harsh times of winter, living prey occupies a smaller proportion of the total diet. By late summer the balance is different. The main items of food are of both animal and vegetable origin. During the summer and autumn badgers eat wild fruits and berries in substantial quantities. Elderberries, frequently found around the sett area, are eaten in season and blackberries are also taken during autumn, usually in large amounts. Various roots and tubers also form part of the diet. Mortimer Batten referred more than once to the badger's fondness for wild hyacinth bulbs,[2] even stating that the animal was prepared to travel two or three miles to obtain such bulbs.

In winter when nature's fruits and berries are unobtainable and when the ground may be iron-hard a good deal of grass is likely to be eaten. Dr Neal and others have noted that grass had been eaten in a number of cases where post-mortems were carried out. I doubt if such food is greatly enjoyed.

Even with an abundance and variety of easily available vegetable matter a badger will still seek out meat or animal food. Many naturalists believe that the earthworm is perhaps the badger's most usual and basic food. I would not disagree, particularly if ground insects, beetles and slugs are added. Nevertheless, important as these animal substances are, the badger favours the flesh of other mammals. Considerable numbers of voles and many mice are eaten, particularly the young whilst they can be located in their nests.

I have seen a badger dig out and swiftly devour a family of mice, the whole operation occupying an astonishingly brief time from the first suspicion of a prospective meal to its conclusion. First the attentive pause, then a recognition swiftly followed by action. I did not notice whether the tail wagged although this is said to be normal on such occasions.

The same approach is usually adopted in taking young rabbits. Wild rabbits rear their young in underground breeding nests, frequently simply scraped out at the end of a short tunnel. The badger may smell the existence of a nest from above, then dig directly down to the tiny rabbits. This is not an invariable practice for often the rabbits may be detected at the entrance of the short excavation and the badger will then dig towards them from the entrance. Approach is always direct and probably from the point where the smell is discerned.

In many areas since the early 1950s when the spread of myxomatosis massively reduced the rabbit population, badgers will not have been able to eat young rabbit very often. Fresh outbursts of the disease flare up occasionally so that the amount of rabbit has been kept quite low during much of the last two decades. Despite this, in some districts the rabbit has increased markedly and figures more frequently in the badgers' diet today than it did ten or fifteen years ago.

Myxomatosis appears to be killing a smaller number of rabbits each time it appears. This may be due to the build up of resistance or it may be because a considerable proportion of our wild rabbits are spending less time below ground. Not that this is likely to affect the badger since the young rabbits are still equally detectable no matter what the patterns of adult living might be, for nests are almost invariably below ground. Even if surface breeding takes place the badger is no less an agent of control.

Where surface existence is common the badger's role as a

predator can be important, for in this situation the only really practicable methods of drastic reduction in rabbit numbers, through the use of gas or of ferrets, are ineffective. Rabbits are unlikely to be killed in adequate numbers if they are not below ground and therefore extremely vulnerable. The young, though, are likely to be below ground for two or three weeks and therefore are accessible to badgers. Thus the economic value of badgers could well be increased as the prevalence of myxomatosis reduces.

Where the rabbit population is again significant the use of snares may become more extensive. Those seeking proper control of rabbits by this means should not, of course, use snares which could take or injure badgers. Often, however, the trapper visiting his snares may well find that a badger has been before him and taken the rabbit. In fact, the taking of snared adults may be the most frequent way by which the badger can consume healthy and well-grown rabbits.

Hares are much less likely to fall victim to badgers for the baby hare is born in a much more advanced condition than the rabbit. The leveret is furred and sighted at birth and mobile at a very early age whilst the rabbit is naked, blind and essentially a young of the nest for some time after its birth. The only hares likely to be eaten by badgers are those which have been snared or injured.

During the seasons when there is abundance in their numbers rabbits and the smaller rodents inevitably provide an important part of the badger's diet. So, in the years of vole 'plagues' not only birds like the short-eared owl feed well but the hunting mammals, too. At other times the proportion of food accounted for by any of these species may be quite low. In the year of the crash following a rodent population explosion the badger diet will be markedly different in its content.

The mole population has grown surprisingly high in some areas in recent years, and moles may provide the badger with occasional meals. This might compensate for the regrettable decline in the frog population, a decline due to many factors including pollution, pond drainage and the disturbance and destruction of natural habitat by modern agricultural methods. Frogs are now eaten much less by predators than they were a few years ago, and the decline of the frog could possibly exert almost as serious an influence upon the activity of some species as the virtual disappearance of the rabbit was expected to do twenty years ago. When a badger does take frogs it is likely to scrub or effectively skin the creatures by a rapid scraping of its claws.

Hedgehogs too are in decline, hundreds being killed daily upon our roads during much of the year. Thus another source of food for the badger is less often encountered. Apart from man, the badger and some foxes are really the hedgehog's only major predators. I have never seen the remains of a hedgehog after a badger has made a meal of it, but there are a number of records that the spines are left upon a flattened skin which is unrolled from the flesh. Similarly the badger usually leaves most of the rabbit's skin which is often also turned inside out, although baby rabbits and smaller creatures are eaten almost whole.

Fairfax Blakeborough believed that badgers would sometimes eat fox cubs and provided some evidence to substantiate this view.[25] Yet this seems to prove only that the badger will attack cubs when the impact of a high local fox population is extensive or where there is seen to be menace and particular interference from the fox. There is certainly no evidence that it is normal for fox and badger to come into conflict. Indeed, foxes very frequently make use of setts, often active ones, for breeding or refuge without arousing hostility. Both predators appear to leave their neighbours alone and, where a sett is shared, quite different and separate chambers are used.

In some areas it is still suspected that badgers kill and eat lambs. There is scarcely any real evidence to support this view but proof seems never to have been essential in the formulation of rural suspicions of this kind. Over half a century ago Mortimer Batten quoted incidents which appear to provide some, if strictly speaking circumstantial, evidence of lamb-killing. One or two lambs were said to have been killed early this century at Lastingham whilst one blood-stained badger was killed near a newly killed lamb in North Wales before World War I. Batten reported people saying that lamb killing was more frequent in earlier years.[2]

Slowly however, the realisation is gaining ground that the badger is not prone to this sort of harmful behaviour. The belief now is that if any lamb is eaten by badgers then it may have been killed by other predators or, more likely, that it died from natural causes.

Badgers do eat carrion. I deliberately left one or two freshly shot wood pigeons near a sett four or five years ago which were taken by badgers. I know, too, that rabbits which have been shot have also been eaten. This appears to support my view that the badger will eat fresh meat quite eagerly. Whether it will readily take more matured carrion cannot yet be proved. Unlike the fox it may be rather more reluctant to eat meat which is not particularly fresh. Batten quoted one case where a captive badger refused to touch a dead lamb but escaped and killed a hen in a nearby coop, and another where stale meat went untouched by a pair of young badgers which ate nothing in a filthy den of captivity and died. One captive badger, though, is said to have been fed entirely on fish and to have looked extremely well![2]

Some of those hostile to the species object to the badger because they consider that as a member of the weasel family it must pose a serious threat to game. I cannot claim that the badger will never take a game bird, its young or its eggs, but I do know of a case, and similar ones have been recorded, where a hen pheasant has raised its brood in close proximity to an occupied sett. A badger is likely to eat eggs and chicks if it stumbles across them, yet overall the effect of badgers on game interests appears to be slight. I consider that the maximum effect exercised by any badgers upon local game interest cannot really account for more than one per cent of reserves. Badgers are un-

Page 61   (*above*) First emergence; (*below*) a typical sett

Page 62 (*above*) Almost fully grown cubs at play, aged about seven months; (*below*) boar and sow grooming each other

Page 63   An energetic scratch!

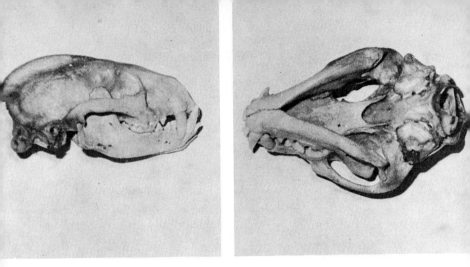

Page 64 (*above*) The skull of a badger, possibly a female. Notice the central ridge of bone which overhangs the base, giving a large measure of protection against head blows. The right-hand picture gives a good view of the jaw which, being almost completely enclosed at the joint, is practically impossible to dislocate; (*below*) the hog or sand badger which comes from southern Asia and has a pig-like appearance

likely to take any of the healthy birds involved or more than a tiny proportion of the total eggs laid or young hatched in any season.

No doubt the badger will take a freshly killed or injured creature, which may not be an irrelevant habit as far as game interests are concerned.

Many of those who own a gun—I do myself—are conscious that where their target is a living creature they have a serious moral responsibility to ensure that death is inflicted without suffering. Unfortunately some of those who shoot either care not at all or are incapable of accuracy, so that quite large numbers of birds and animals are left to die. If the badger encounters such a creature naturally it will kill and eat it. Not acting from any sense of compassion the badger will have served a purpose welcome to many by scavenging after that kind of sportsman who really ought not to be allowed to possess anything larger than a pea shooter.

Lest any reader doubts the justification for that comment, I am informed by the most reliable sources that inspection of hind carcasses shot by the very competent or the professional in winter and of stag carcasses shot by some holidaying sportsmen might well reveal not only a noticeable difference in marksmanship, but that hinds suffer a great deal less than many stags. The deer, though a larger target than the badger, in some ways is warier and more agile. Yet it still receives unnecessary wounds and it has not been unknown for badgers to be the targets of irresponsible shots. I know that near one sett which I have often watched an adult badger was shot by someone who mistook it for a rabbit in the open! That badger died quite quickly. Many others may not have been so fortunate for a shotgun is not the ideal weapon with which to kill badgers, particularly if it is used at any distance with light shot. The badger is a stout animal. If wounded it is likely to struggle back to its sett and might suffer for a long time before death.

Lack of knowledge, and the employment as gamekeepers of men with only rearing ability, could well be of great disadvantage to the badger which offers little harm to them and may be most useful. It is more likely to eat a dead or injured pheasant than a healthy one and will more than compensate by its other choices of food. Also where there is a substantial badger population their nightly wanderings are likely to ensure that pheasants roost above ground, as proved by Philip Drabble's recorded observations.[6] It is possible that the odd pheasant may be taken by an opportunistic badger but the compulsion to roost above ground springing from badgers' presence in the locality is likely to provide a significant net gain for the shooting interest.

The badger as a poultry killer is a complex issue. In past decades, even though poultry killing by badgers was said to be extensive, it is probable that the great majority of badgers never tasted domestic fowl. Today the number of badgers which have eaten this food is likely to be tiny.

The principal reason for this is not that the badger has been redeemed from a life of crime but simply that farming methods have changed. The farmer's wife does not usually now take responsibility for the flock of hens living around the farm house nor is she economically dependent upon them. Today poultry is generally kept on a large scale in purpose-built units which, if properly maintained, prevent badgers from getting at the birds inside. A few hens may still be killed by badgers but such losses will be extremely small. If any farmer feels that retribution is needed he could well reflect that the little harm thus caused is greatly outweighed by the badger's eating of other pests, which inevitably saves crops from a greater degree of damage or destruction.

I believe that badgers offer little threat to poultry. Dr Neal provided further confirmation of this view when he referred to the experience of Mr Howard Lancum of the Ministry of Agriculture who found the badger guilty in only two out of 100 cases investigated where a badger was thought to be involved in poultry killing.[19]

Few people have watched a badger eating. It appears to take favoured food with a salivating relish, quickly, but not with any remarkably ravening swiftness. Half-a-century ago Batten wrote that where there is an abundance of food the badger will gorge itself to repletion and then spend a very long period in its sett, not to reappear for three or four nights unless it be to use the nearby dung-pits, when 'the amount of excrement in one night at such times passes all belief'.[2] I cannot agree with that conclusion. Like most predators, the badger's digestive juices and arrangements are such as will not allow any feeling of satisfaction to persist for such a great length of time. Of course, badger survival can be managed without large and regular meals. Wild carnivores do not become accustomed to three or four meals every twenty-four hours.

How then does the badger obtain food? Leaving the sett it walks steadily along one of its well-trodden paths, usually into the wind. No doubt it may head in a direction recently taken when it was fortunate enough to locate enjoyed food. It may well walk towards water, possibly because food is a little more likely to be found near water than not. In areas of established coniferous woodland it is reasonable to suppose that the badger will walk either towards the edge of the wood or to a ride rather than into the heart of the plantation where little sustenance is likely to be found. As it moves along the badger is attentive to the chances of food and sometimes takes a mouthful of corn in passing. Away from the sett, it is usually much less suspicious than other species of wild mammals being far more concerned with finding food, although it remains alert for others of its species.

I have followed badgers on summer evenings and watched them eat, but I have not been so fortunate as Arthur Killingley, the Mammal Society County Recorder for Buckinghamshire, who has described a most interesting experience when he followed a young badger and closely observed it eating slugs. The animal stopped for such a meal on thirty-two occasions during a period of about a couple of hours.[14]

It is, of course, quite impossible to record full details of the badger's diet from observation of the animal in the wild. Most of its feeding occurs during hours of darkness, often in quite thick cover. Occasional experiences when an individual is observed feeding may provide some entertaining information and confirm a little of the knowledge otherwise deduced. It may be possible to form some conclusions from observation of badgers kept in domesticity, although I gather the only firm conclusion so far reached is that such animals can have very hearty appetites indeed. And, since the badger is almost omnivorous, a study of the healthy captives is not likely to provide definite information as to the habits and diets of the wild creature. Patterns of life and opportunity inevitably differ. Indeed, I rather think that one could maintain a badger on breakfast cereals and dog food.

It is for this reason that the studies of badger diet based upon analysis of droppings have been valuable. Such analysis confirms that the variety of foods consumed is very wide and also that the earthworm is a major or staple item. Seasonal and regional fluctuations seem also to be proved.

On grounds of nutrition it seems sure that good health is not generally at risk, but it is well to remember that health and vigour are not only determined by diet and that the environment is also most relevant. Where the sett is dry the badger's physical condition is likely to be healthier than in a damp situation. A sett in sand, which is naturally preferred, is more likely to be healthier than one in clay. The oldest badgers appear to live in dry and secure setts.

Dr Neal has quoted the comments of Miss Frances Pitt and Sir Frederick Hobday in regard to a form of acute tonsillitis which had severe effect.

Even in old age badgers' teeth are normally in quite remarkably good condition which is fortunate as dental disease can be serious. Dr Paget has studied the skulls and teeth of many badgers and noticed areas of osteo-myelitis usually in clear association with dental disease. An examination of one young badger which apparently died of starvation showed a broken pre-molar which led to abscess development. It is assumed that

acute pain would have been caused by this condition particularly when biting. No doubt this led to the fatal starvation.[21]

There are a few districts today where badgers are free from
molestation so that natural existence is possible. In such places
the badger might last as long as its teeth. These seem not to be
given to early or rapid decay and thus an age of ten years or
more is by no means impossible. Some wild badgers do die of
old age perhaps passing their tenth year, while in captivity they
often live for another two or three years. No doubt greater
ages than ten years have been attained in the wild although the
average life span is bound to be very much less even in un-
harassed setts. Mortality may be due more to injury than to
disease.

Given the limitation of underground and wild existence
badgers are clean animals. This may be one important reason
for the assumption that the badger is normally healthy and for
the fact that long and full life is possible.

This view of the badger's health and cleanliness has not always
been held. Turberville maintained that it was necessary to wash
one's hands after touching the badger for the animal was then
said to be disease-ridden. A form of mange affecting badgers
was thought to be very common indeed.[30] There is no evidence
that any such disease is common in Britain today or that it has
been in the recent past.

Diseases do affect badgers, but they are unlikely to spread
with speed or rapidly to assume epidemic proportions. Obviously, if one animal has an infection this might easily and
quickly spread to those animals within its own family, particularly where they currently occupy the same sett, but the
territorial consciousness of the species would restrict infection
or at least reduce the possibility of rapidity in contagion.

In the 1800s and in the early part of the twentieth century the
badger population is likely to have been much lower than it is
today. This may have been largely due to the poverty of the
peasant, to the cause of game preservation and different agricultural activity or poultry rearing practice, and it is reasonable to

assume that few badgers survived for anything like the normal life span.

This view is supported by Richard Jefferies' comment in 1878: 'Here in the furze too is the haunt of the badger. This animal becomes rarer year after year—the disuse of the great rabbit-warrens being one cause; still he lingers, and may be traced in the rabbit "burries", where he enlarges a hole for his habitation sleeps during the day, and comes forth in the gloaming.'[12]

Jefferies revealed a close knowledge of most wild creatures. The somewhat less than accurate nature of his deductions and relatively sparse comment concerning the badger seem to confirm the relative scarcity of the species in his day. As we know, the badger is not dependent upon rabbit 'burries' although frequently one can see enlargement of burrows during the practice diggings and excavations which are part of the young badger's apprenticeship.

It is possible that there were more badgers last century than people imagined. I was chatting the other day to one experienced farmer with a very wholesome attitude towards wildlife who confessed that he had never seen a wild badger. Whilst there are no setts on his farm I know two within a short distance of it. Such a situation is not at all unusual and lack of sighting rather than actual absence may have been the case in the past leading to the conclusion of scarcity. Certainly, when coupled with the more destructive interest in natural history in the last century this lack of sightings does seem to support the assumption that the population was smaller.

Badgers may suffer from lung complaints peculiar to the species including a form of tuberculosis, in addition to the very occasional and isolated infection by the bovine strain. In the last few years a good deal of evidence has been provided to show that a few badgers have contracted this type of tuberculosis in one or two localities. It is not suggested that this infection has been contracted or transmitted in any wide area or upon any large scale. However, it received some public attention during the summer of 1973 when the Badgers Act was before Parliament, and subsequently as a result of research and surveys on behalf of the Ministry of Agriculture. During a debate on the Bill however, assurance was given that those badgers proved to be carrying the disease would not be protected for the wrong reasons. At that time I pointed out that: 'a number of people hold the view that the badger, whilst carrying bovine tuberculosis, is scarcely likely to infect other species. Certainly it is likely that the badger has picked up tuberculosis from infected cattle, because it wanders along the pastures on which the cattle graze, eating slugs and so on. However, the badger itself, in performing its ablutions, is uniquely hygienic. It invariably uses dung-pits, which are generally very close to the sett. Because it uses dung pits, the likelihood of cattle contracting the disease from badgers is much smaller than the likelihood of badgers contracting the disease from cattle'.[10]

Further consideration does not lead me to change the view expressed. It is a fact, of course, that in two areas where the badger population is very high and where setts are close to pasture some of the animals have contracted and carry bovine tuberculosis. In Gloucestershire bovine tuberculosis in cattle was found in some younger beasts and it was suspected that the cause might lie in the area's wildlife. The badger population there is, or was, extremely dense. R. H. Muirhead stated that in the area involved 32 setts had been identified with an estimated population of at least 300 badgers. This estimate seems a little high unless many setts have not been located, since a population of ten badgers per sett is extremely unusual even in this district of sandstone and woodland which is ideal badger country. In this area four badgers were found to be infected with bovine tuberculosis in 1971 and three of these were considered to be infective in the ways which could lead to the contamination of pasture. The great majority of the local badgers studied were free from the disease.[18]

In the other area where this phenomenon has occurred, near West Penwith in Cornwall, a survey was conducted based upon analysis of 49 badgers and 53 samples of faeces. Tubercle bacilli were identified in three of the samples each from fairly closely adjacent setts. Evidence was there, and the farmers near the setts involved were advised to consult the Ministry's officers. In the interest of the species as a whole eradication at the actual setts involved could not be condemned. In those localities affected the hard and stern action which has been taken seems quite unavoidable.

In May 1974 I accompanied Roland Moyle, Parliamentary Secretary, Ministry of Agriculture, on a visit to a Gloucestershire farm. Several herds of cattle had had to be destroyed in the area and in every case the evidence, circumstantial though it was, made it entirely clear that the badgers there must be destroyed. On this occasion there was some criticism of the methods employed by the Ministry's officials by which the badgers were shot, snared or trapped. In this case I consider the control was as humane as possible.

Although gassing would be the best means of control it is still illegal to gas badgers, a point which I have taken up with the Minister, urging him to take the necessary powers to allow gas to be used by licensing his officers or other responsible persons. A blanket power is unnecessary and gas should be used against badgers only in those few localities where it is necessary.

The Gloucestershire visit confirmed my view that the situation there was not typical of most of the rest of Britain as the badger population was obviously unusually dense.

There is, therefore, no justification for widespread destruction since this disease appears to be restricted to animals in those areas where unique conditions exist. Of course, the longevity of the particular bacilli contributes to the problem.

I must stress that there is no evidence so far to suggest that this phenomenon is other than very localised. It cannot be denied that the badger has transmitted the disease; indeed, in one or two cases no other explanation is possible. However, tests reveal that in other and similar areas where setts can be found near pasture it is very clear that there is no risk of harm whatsoever.

CHAPTER 5

THE SETT

The badger has long been adapted to a subterranean day. Long ago it may not have lived below ground. Then, no doubt because of experience of insecurity, longer residence developed. Today perhaps two-thirds of a badger's life is spent in its underground home, the sett.

Given the vicious treatment which badgers have generally received from man it is not surprising that they have sought safety in extensive habitation below ground. Many setts have been occupied for generations and each of these may have developed the underground workings further. Some long-established ones have become so sizeable that we cannot easily assess their structure. I should think the actual size and pattern of the largest sett in Britain would be seen as quite astonishing. It is likely that workings at the largest setts extend over an area of a couple of hundred square yards and along possibly more than a mile of underground tunnels between a variety of exits and into many excavated chambers. Of course, a lot of the old workings might have collapsed for not all could ever be in

E

current use, but it is evident that work in a sett is never complete so that passages and chambers are continually being opened and reopened.

Evidence that work is continuous is provided by the heaps of excavated earth which are thrown from setts. Fresh ones are usually to be found at any active sett. Often I have visited a sett in the evening and seen freshly ejected earth so that we may be mistaken if we imagine that badgers are in continuous sleep when below ground. Much subterranean day-time activity certainly occurs.

Because of the setts' nature we can know very little about them. Sometimes setts are little more than occupations of underground space and fissures which may have been naturally created and such homes are certainly to be found in rocky and mountainous areas. Mostly, however, the underground chambers in which badgers sleep have been dug out by themselves. Indeed, the badger needs no other excavator for it has adequately evolved the necessary skill and capacity. It is said that the badger can dig as much in one night as any strong man. The badger has an innate determination to dig and is never quite satisfied with existing accommodation.

At first a sett may be merely a small sleeping space at the end of a short tunnel but the badger will not be satisfied with this for long. First, another tunnel leading to a second exit will be excavated, then other chambers, and the tunnels between them will be dug and fresh entrances opened. In areas where the badgers have long been established these underground workings will be extensive offering many exits, not all of which will be in use during any one season. At one sett I know that a total of twenty-four holes have been used in the last seven years but, at any time, not more than four or five have been in use.

One general practice is that whilst the badger, in emergency, will enter the sett by any open hole it is usual for one exit only to be used by a particular animal or family for a period. Yet air may often be tested from more than one hole prior to emergence. On a recent visit to one sett I was told that a particular exit was being used by the sow and her cubs. It was, but before the sett was vacated the sow's head appeared to be assessing the air at another entrance some yards away. I doubt if a second check is made unless grounds for suspicion have developed.

I suppose that the choice of entrance may depend upon the position of the currently favoured sleeping chambers. The sow may choose to rear her cubs in a new chamber and make use of a new or re-opened entrance. Where a particularly suitable and secure chamber exists this is likely to be used rather than an entirely new one, but new quarters are being opened up all the time.

Frequently the position of the main entrances seem to show some evidence of caution or good sense. Often holes are close to the best natural approach to the sett and to the path of the prevailing wind so that detection of hostility is facilitated. I do not suggest that deliberate planning or selection of position for reasons of security is invariable or usual but it appears to be more than coincidental at certain setts. The hole which is used for emergence is not at all certain to be the one used for descent nor for the movement of bedding. Sometimes bedding as well as excavation or deliberate obstruction partially block a hole to make it temporarily unusable for exit or entrance. There is, of course, considerable variation in setts and in the activity within them. Clearly each family adapts to its own environment.

Badgers reveal proprietorial characteristics in their territory and cling to long-established setts. Often features which assist security are utilised. Sometimes the breeding or sleeping chambers may be situated under trees or large rocks for defence purposes. Often, too, there are varying levels within the sett which may provide an advantage over intruders. In rocky areas this sort of arrangement may be particularly frequent.

It is thought that a sett may provide accommodation and tunnels at two levels, that there may be galleries within the sett. This may be so where natural rock formation encourages it, particularly in rather steeply sloping areas, but I rather think that different 'floors' may be unusual and where they do occur they are probably not in regular and current use. Of course, there may well be a difference in levels between the tunnel and the living chamber to enhance security. Any other animal entering the sett and offering a threat underground would be at a marked disadvantage when approaching a badger occupying a higher position. Mortimer Batten described a sett near Bolton Abbey in Yorkshire where the chamber in occupation was at a higher level than the tunnel leading towards it. Two terriers were killed in that sett and the defence advantage might have been a very important factor in the badger's victory.

The tunnels in a sett will normally be just under 1ft wide. However, the sleeping chambers are likely to be at least 4ft long, 1½ft high and 2½ or 3ft wide. Usually the ceiling of such a chamber will not be less than 4ft below the surface, perhaps more than twice that depth.

Much depends upon the nature of the soil and rock involved. In highland areas natural cavities may allow very deep chambers to be used although great depth is unlikely since it would be excessively cold and damp. In low-lying land anything other than shallow occupation may be out of the question because of inadequate drainage and the level of the water table, and this in turn may limit the number of setts which can be excavated. It is likely that this is the major reason for the scarcity of the species in certain localities in the Eastern counties where flat, open and marshy land is usual. Suitable situations are not easily found in fenland areas and it is unlikely that a dense population has ever existed or could do so in these districts. In such areas badger colonies utilise embankments.

Badgers do not always establish setts in inaccessible or well hidden situations although the favoured sites are those which provide suitable cover. Obviously a wood is the best place for residence since otherwise a long-established sett would become exceedingly obvious. So much earth is thrown out that the holes are surrounded by raised ground. Frequently long ridges of earth are piled out from the sett and within the area of the sett the ground is likely to be trodden bare by nightly movement and play. A well established sett is generally quite easily seen unless dense seasonal vegetation surrounds it.

In summer, however, even in relatively open situations, established setts may be hidden by certain plants which seem to thrive above them. Nettles often grow tall and in thick profusion as do elders, which have spread to become the dominant vegetation around many setts. No doubt this is because the soil in the vicinity of a sett is rich in nitrogen.

At the time of writing, most of the dozen setts nearest my home are exceedingly difficult to watch because of thick, in some cases almost impenetrable, vegetation. Some setts may be very difficult to locate during summer months particularly because of such thick seasonal vegetation. Discovery is usually possible if badger paths are followed. One drawback is, of course, that a path may be taken away from a sett rather than towards it! Usually several clearly visible paths radiate irregularly from any established sett. Normally a path in regular use is likely to be seen easily. Of course, the badger will proceed under obstacles which are a barrier to man and in thick vegetation the path may seem to be more of a tunnel seven or eight inches wide and little more than one foot high. Many paths gradually fade out as use becomes irregular at increasing distances from the sett since badgers leave their paths wherever they may be tempted to do so.

There are well trodden paths to badgers' dung-pits which are usually near the sett although this is not always the case. One summer evening when I was searching for a sett I found several dung-pits but no sett, nor was there one nearby. Perhaps where considerable distances are covered pits may be used well away from the sett. This may be true where the sett is some way from water as the badger may take a long time to reach water after leaving the sett and a distant dung-pit may be used.

Journeys are not one of continuous movement by any means. The badger pauses frequently to musk stones, stumps, posts and so on as territorial and route markers. Of course, it will stop to eat when food is located, to satisfy curiosity or even visit other setts en route whether active or disused, and will often be a considerable distance away from its own sett for a long period so that it is not really surprising that sometimes dung-pits exist far from the 'home' ones.

The usual dung-pit is quite small, not much more than 5in deep. It is roughly circular in shape, with a diameter of about 5 or 6in. Usually the pit is filled, then left and a new one is dug. Several open ones are often to be seen at the same time and close together. I have not noticed any evidence that each is the strict property of one animal although this is possible. I do not think that badgers cover used dung-pits. Obviously space is filled as leaves, sticks and decaying vegetation cover the wood floor.

Just as the dung-pit is evidence of badger occupation so is the existence of a scratching post which I mentioned earlier. Observation of grooming and of the use of a scratching post reveals that the badger expends considerable energy in this activity so that eventually if a tree is long used it may be completely spoilt or badly damaged (see page 90). I recently timed a badger carrying out grooming after emergence and there was almost incessant scratching and rubbing for just over fifteen minutes. Imagine the effect upon the scratching tree if one animal were to rub upon it for a quarter-of-an-hour every evening throughout its life. If each badger at the sett uses the same tree or post as often seems to be the case, it is not surprising that the effect upon a selected tree is very obvious.

The Mammal Society's survey[16] shows that deciduous woods or mixed woods are more favoured than the dense conifer plantations. This is not surprising for under the thick conifer canopy other vegetation is inhibited so that an adequate variety of abundant natural life cannot be sustained and a substantial badger population could scarcely thrive. This is hardly an argument against afforestation for there are relatively few areas where this effect is likely to be experienced even if, as is desirable for so many reasons, a larger national planting programme is pursued. If conifer plantation is unattractive in terms of adequate natural balance the current concern for environment will not allow the absolute obliteration of natural features and wildlife. The areas likely to be newly and densely planted are generally not ones which support a heavy badger population although greater afforestation might more seriously affect a few other species of our fauna. On the other hand balanced planting programmes would reduce such harm by the provision of cyclical opportunity within any forest area.

Less than one sett in fourteen is to be found to be in coniferous woods. Well over half our setts appear to be in deciduous or mixed woods and copses although many of the widely afforested counties have not yet been thoroughly surveyed.

It might seem that woodland badgers' activities are inimical to good forestry but this is not necessarily true. Although new plantation may be impossible in the actual area of the sett itself, such waste of land is relatively small. Often, too, the site favoured by the badger may be of little value for forestry, at the side of a steep slope perhaps. In one wood which I know well, the total area of land dominated by three setts is less than 500sq yd and almost all of this is scarcely suitable for trees. This situation is hardly severe in land-use costs, particularly in view of the limitation provided by the badgers on the rodent population which may be a problem to both neighbouring agricultural as well as forestry interests.

Of all the South Yorkshire setts three-quarters are in woodland or hedgerows with three in disused quarries and two are in an open position. I quote my local area as the balance of sett distribution here seems very similar to the national position as shown in the Mammal Society's records.[16] Of course, my locality does not include any heath or moorland and in these areas the proportion of setts in open country is clearly higher.

In areas with a reasonable proportion of woodland relatively few of the setts will lie far from the wood's edge and a majority will almost certainly be situated less than 60yd from it. Frequently setts so situated are large and, therefore, long established. These may be so extensive that a single large sett may appear to be two separate ones. At one large sett which has often been disturbed I have noticed that badgers test the air before emergence at two holes 30yd apart.

At the wood with three setts previously mentioned the two smaller ones are about 100yd apart and 70 and 90yd from the main sett, indicating that sett distribution is not designed with any view of apportionment of territory. The choice of a sett seems more likely to be dictated by reasons of security, structural suitability and family sociability where any possibility of a choice of sites does exist.

Quite a lot of setts are found in hedgerows particularly where the hedge is thick and upon a bank, and almost one sett in ten is described as being in an open situation. This may mean that the badgers concerned have clung to their sett despite considerable change in their environment. Sometimes the nature of the locality is changed so that what may once have been a secluded and peaceful home is no longer so secure. Yet it may be inhabited long after the change occurred, which may explain the origin of some setts in open country.

There is one occupied sett, for example, in my constituency which is within a short stone-throw of a motorway. Badgers may not remain there permanently but there is no sign of abandonment and it is five years since the motorway was opened. Another sett in an open position has been there as long as local memory.

This tenacity of tenure was noted by various County Recorders carrying out the Badger Survey. They revealed that badgers do not leave their territory in the face of encroaching man which is why they can be found within or very near conurbations. Where men are close neighbours badgers probably stay underground a little later in the day but they will remain in the locality. It is rather surprising then that such badgers are not more often seen: once away from the sett the animal can be comparatively nonchalant in its disregard of observers as some of those who feed badgers in their gardens have realised.

Possibly the removal of hedgerows—2,500 miles have been

cleared in England over a 10 year period—has created the open situation in which a number of setts are found. Such hedgerows provide a habitat for a multitude of wild creatures, including forty or more kinds of birds and, of course, at least 100 species of wild plants which are located in and dependent upon hedgerows. There is a danger that so many wild plants will disappear that adequate variety in the world's botanical reserves will cease to exist, so reducing our long-term capacity to rely upon the resilience of nature.

Badgers frequently inhabit disused quarries which may offer natural cavities and fissures, and often very suitable cover flourishes following the end of the quarry's working. The soil and rock of such an area is also likely to be suitable for the badger certainly prefers stone to mud. Only a small proportion of setts are to be found in clay but about half the setts surveyed are in sandy soil which is easily worked, so that it is not surprising that many extensive setts are to be found in sandstone regions. Yet this ease of excavation may not be the only reason why setts are often found in old quarries. Wherever possible the badger will make its home in sandy soil below hard stone, a preference which can be satisfied in many quarries. These conditions are often encountered in areas of heavy badger population including both the Cotswolds and Somerset.

Most of our badgers dig their setts on land 100ft above sea level and much low-lying land is ruled out as a badger habitat, but the badger cannot be regarded as a highland animal. Relatively few setts are to be found over 700–800ft above sea level. The highest known in England is below 2,000ft, and whilst there may be one or two setts higher than this in Wales or the Scottish Highlands, only a tiny proportion of Britain's badgers live in mountainous areas.

One advantage of a hill-dwelling badger is that it can live in sloping land. Level ground is not favoured as a rule and most setts are dug into slopes. The advantages are clear, drainage is better, the soil which is excavated can more easily be thrown out of the way, and suitable strata can be located and worked more easily.

I suppose that sloping land with sandy soil, under a limestone outcrop, in deciduous woodland with good ground cover could be regarded as the ideal. If, in addition, the area was undisturbed and, further, if the entrances faced south then the badgers would probably regard the situation as perfect. Any sett in such a situation may well have accommodated badgers for many generations, perhaps for centuries.

Many believe that the badger's sett is ideally located near a stream. I am by no means sure of this. At one sett I know a site nearer water could easily have been chosen. At another, despite the existence of steep slopes at either side of a small stream not far within the wood, that immediate locality is ignored and the setts are sited almost 100yd away. In this case both positions are at a similar distance from the side of a wood.

Like almost all predators the badger swims naturally: as a relative of the otter this is not at all surprising. Water may be used at times for immersion as a relief from insect parasites in the same manner as the fox, although this is by no means established as a recognised common practice. I suppose that if a sett is near relatively deep water it is likely that immersion is a more common experience than it is for most animals, although it is certain that many badgers never swim at all.

Badgers drink water regularly, but I do not believe that the badger needs to drink very copiously and while I have seen eager satisfaction of thirst, I have equally watched badgers leave their sett at dusk and cross a small stream with only a slight pause for a drink. In dry weather the badger may well take most of its liquid intake indirectly in its food although it has been known to visit farms and drink from cattle troughs.

Another practice which may be much more common than is generally supposed is that of sleeping above ground. This has long been known but its incidence is not really established. Batten quoted one story of foxhounds encountering two badgers which were sleeping in bracken,[2] stretched out nose to tail, when the hounds descended and killed them.

Batten also described one occasion when, in broad daylight, he noticed bedding above a sett arranged as if it were a couch. Hurrying to fetch a camera he found on his return that the bedding was gone. He advanced this experience as evidence that badgers not only will sleep above ground but bring out bedding for this purpose.

I take the view that very few badgers sleep above ground permanently. Many do so from time to time but I doubt if the bringing out of bedding is common. I have disturbed badgers during the day on several occasions; on two of these the badgers have been lying on bare earth and several times I have noticed them move from a small area of very flattened bracken. Most but by no means all such occurrences have been in the summer. It could be that in summer months when the sett is surrounded by dense vegetation of a variety not favoured for bedding the collection, and particularly the movement to the sett of fresh and dry bedding in substantial quantity, might be difficult. That this difficulty induces some badgers to bring their bedding out for airing is a possibility I suppose, but I should like to see further real evidence.

It may be argued that bedding is brought out for a few hours at colder periods when bare earth is less inviting. At such times however, the badger's coat is likely to be at its most dense so the necessity for surface bedding is scarcely essential. In any case I think that sleeping in an exposed position in cold weather is rather unlikely. In very cold wintry weather badgers may congregate in family groups for mutual comfort.

Tests of sett temperatures have been taken below ground by means of lowered thermometers. These reveal that the chambers are by no means so uncomfortable as one might imagine. Badgers sleeping close together may generate an appreciable warmth so that they generally enjoy air at well above ground-level temperature. In such a situation sleeping above ground will not be much of a temptation.

Very occasionally evidence of surface residence occurs. Dr Neal has described one case when a sow was found to be rearing cubs in a farm building in Somerset. The litter occupied a substantial nest. We cannot know the reason for such isolated examples of unusual behaviour. In this case the sow could have produced her litter at the farm or moved it there as a result of interference or destruction at her chosen quarters. The arrangement is likely to have been made hastily. If so then it suggests that one view, once commonly held, that sow badgers can postpone parturition is not really tenable now.

Sometimes rabbits or foxes share the badger's sett. This is not to suggest that the creatures live happily together. Rabbits will certainly occupy a different part of the sett, possibly one no longer used by the badgers.

The fox's occupation of part of a sett is most often to be noticed during the late winter and early spring. Quite frequently a large sett may accommodate a litter of fox cubs and one of badgers at the same time. But the fox and the badger do not share a small sett or the same part of a large one, possibly because the fox is by no means so fastidious a creature; a fox's occupancy can be detected easily for a powerful and offensive smell is evident. The fox takes food to the sett which contributes to the stink that is especially penetrating if the entrance is at all close to the chamber in which fox cubs have been reared.

Often the badger is blamed for the depredations of a fox. If chickens are stolen and remains are found outside a sett then the badger rather than the fox may receive the odium. In fact, for a badger to take food back to or into the sett is abnormal behaviour and I have never seen any evidence of it. Usually the badger eats as it finds. As a general rule, the remains of food near a sett is evidence of a fox's visit or occupancy and not that of even the rare and unacceptable rogue badger.

It is interesting to watch a sett occupied currently by both species. I have never seen either acknowledge the other. At one of the two large setts I know which are often shared the fox does not loiter about the sett for very long, but is away from the close locality with its cubs below ground when the badgers appear. In late summer I have counted fifteen minutes elapse between the departure of a dog fox and the emergence of the first badger, usually the boar.

I was extremely fortunate on one occasion when I had taken a position quite close to a hole from which I expected badgers to emerge. A very slight breeze was blowing towards me. After about twenty minutes a fox emerged from another entrance which I had ignored and which was too far away for me to have discerned the usually pungent odour. The fox moved away for four or five yards quite quickly and then ambled off at an angle of 45 degrees from me, pausing several times. Just over fifteen minutes later the first badger appeared, immediately followed by two others. They emerged from another hole which I had not expected to be used, which was three or four yards from the exit chosen by the fox. They did not leave the sett area so quickly as the fox although they did not stay for as long as I had anticipated, for normally at this sett there is a good deal of activity before departure.

The particular sett described is a large one with thirteen open holes. As I write this chapter, four of the holes have appeared or been re-opened in the last few months and one other which was blocked by wood and large stones has been used since I re-opened it recently. The sett stretches about 15yd in one direction and 30yd in the other. One obvious piece of evidence as to the age of this sett is the fact that several of the entrances are actually quite deep at the base of the funnel-shaped basins gradually created by long use of these entrances. Interestingly, all but three of the holes at this sett are in quite level ground only a short distance from the top of a slight ridge. Normally most of the entrances would have been on the side of the slope so close by. It is at least possible that this was the case originally and that the level entrances suggest that the actual underground quarters are rather deep. In addition the existing entrances may be much better places for receiving scent than they would be if they were a few feet further into the wood in the slope which faces the interior. Certainly this is a very adequate reason for the present position and the level approach to most holes. However, on many visits I have seen the first appearance, if not the emergence, at one of the entrances on the slope. This sett has often been attacked by diggers. Perhaps they followed the advice of Turberville who considered the sett in terms of medieval defence.[30]

Indeed, the approach he advised for an assault upon a sett could almost be equated to the siege of a citadel. He listed the tools for 'five or six strong men' to use and gave other advice so that: 'In this order of battell a noble man or gentleman may march to beseige the fox and badgerd in their strongest holes and castles. And may break their casements, platforms and parapets and work them with mynes and countermynes until they get their skins to make furres and mittens.'

CHAPTER 6

DISTRIBUTION AND POPULATION

Meles meles, the European badger, is found in many areas of Europe and Asia, even at latitudes quite far north where semi-hibernation or periods of long duration within the setts are regarded as normal. It is not the only member of the genus mustelidae as there are several other species in both the New World and the Old. In America, for example, a species of badger (*taxidea taxus*) can be found between Alberta and Central Mexico. This animal usually lives in open country and appears to favour dry areas.

Like our own badger, the American species, whilst basically a carnivore, feeds widely. Slightly smaller than its European counterpart it has grey or reddish-brown hair on the upper parts and is pale below, as opposed to the European badger which has darker hair on the underparts and is more lightly coloured above. The American badger has black markings on the face and throat and behind the ears with a white stripe from the nose to the shoulder. Its coat has often been taken by the fur trade and its hair is or was used for shaving brushes.

The hog or sand badger (*arctonyx collaris*) is found in the southern areas of Asia. This animal has a longer tail than our own species and a hairless, quite long snout which has aptly been described as pig-like. The teledu, otherwise known as the mydaus or stink badger (*mydaus javinsis*), comes from Sumatra, Java and Borneo. The anal glands of this creature have developed so that it can emit a strong and unpleasant smell. Its upper lip is divided and there is a short tail from which a white stripe stretches along the back to the head.

In some islands and on the mainland of south-east Asia lives the ferret badger which has a long tail and a naked snout. There may be three sub-species (*melogate personata, m. moschata, m. orientatis*) but all have a white face with black mask-like markings. These animals are particularly useful since they assist the control of harmful insects.

Another badger-like animal is the ratel or honey badger (*mellivora capensis*) found in Senegal and other parts of Africa. Long thought of as a member of the badger family, in recent years particularly it has come to be regarded as being a separate species. The ratel has grey upper parts with darker, brown or black hair below. Like badgers, the skin is hard and tough and this assists the ratel to feed upon insects and snakes. Indeed, it is said to form a working partnership with the honey guide bird.

The European badger can be found in most parts of Great Britain but density of population varies immensely. Regional populations are, to a large extent, determined by topographical factors already considered. Within any region, of course, the distribution and number of badgers will vary greatly depending upon the attitudes of man. Thus, on certain estates and farms the badger may be tolerated or welcome, on others destroyed whenever it appears. Probably the sort of landlord and game-keeper who continues to use or allow the use of the illegal pole trap will also be more than likely to eradicate badgers whether protective legislation exists or not. It is probably fair to assume that the owner or manager of any estate is aware if traps are

Page 89   (*above*) Badger on a regular track through a wood; (*below*)
fallen trees like this become well-loved playgrounds

Page 90 (above) a sett entrance in everyday use; (below) a damaged tree, worn through constant use as a scratching post

used. This may not be the case if badgers are destroyed for they may be killed in their sett without obvious evidence of destruction. So, the badger may be destroyed at the request of a shooting syndicate or an ill-informed landlord, or without the knowledge of either by the gamekeepers they employ.

Whilst in any region the population of badgers is largely determined by physical conditions, within similar localities density may be extremely varied and sparse numbers may be most of all a result of persecution. Where there is real ignorance or hostility it is likely that the badger population will be quite tiny even though a suitable habitat exists. Man thus causes considerable differences in population between areas which offer apparently identical conditions.

Broadly speaking, most badgers in Britain are found in situations above sea level and not much above the heather line of our highland areas. The main badger area can almost be seen as one stretching in the south from Cornwall to Kent covering the West Midland counties but certainly excluding much of East Anglia and the high Pennine region.

In part of Wales, and Denbigh is certainly one such area, there is a considerable badger population despite the marked hostility in many districts. Indeed, one badger supporter received a letter from Wales suggesting that if badgers were not kept down they could come from their holes and eat children! The highest areas of Wales accommodate relatively few badgers but elsewhere numbers are locally high.

Distribution in Scotland appears to be extremely varied but it is likely that in many areas the population is still increasing, for Scotland has not experienced the end of a period of expansion which has occurred in England and Wales in recent years.

Perhaps more badgers did live in the highlands before the nineteenth century when intense war against everything which might threaten game could well have prevented survival in many districts. Eradication may well have wiped out whole families and cleared territories when sporting activity in Scotland developed from the 1840s.

F

W. H. Pearsall[23] noted that in Glen Garry between 1837–40, 67 badgers were destroyed (as well as 198 wild cats, 106 pole-cats, 246 martens and 48 otters). Whilst gas was not then available snares and traps certainly were and the badger may be snared with relative ease. The destruction of every occupant of a sett by snaring is certainly possible and this sort of activity could well have depleted the numbers of Scottish highland badgers very severely. Yet comparison with the number of other predators killed does suggest that the pre-nineteenth-century badger population in such areas could not have been at all high.

It should be realised that in many areas of the highlands the terrain and vegetation present a scarcely ideal opportunity for the species. One major reason for the recent increase in numbers is the extent of reafforestation. The heavy reliance upon conifer plantation may not be ideal but it does provide the cover around the sett which is normally desired.

The highland areas of England also offer little that is suitable for badgers. Some do wander among the heather but the pro-portion of the British badger population existing in such areas is very small indeed. Similarly, flat, wet land is not generally favoured. Whilst such areas generally support a considerable variety of wildlife and could supply adequate nourishment for badgers there are relatively few places in which setts could be established. As was noted in the previous chapter some low-lying setts do exist in fenland but what setts there are seem likely to be found only on raised ground. In one low-lying area of Yorkshire, for example, the only occupied sett is situated in the bank of a drainage dyke.

Dense industrial conurbations also have little to offer the species. Where badgers have survived the pressures of distur-bance, traffic and persecution it is not possible to be sure that they will continue to do so. Yet it would be wrong to assume that absence or disappearance from cities is inevitable since the badger has clung on in a few setts in Greater London. And there are large numbers of setts in Surrey and Sussex despite the fact that the populations of these and others of the Home Counties have soared. Cotswolds setts are not far from the factories of the West Midlands.

Badger numbers today are still appreciably smaller in the UK than they were less than ten years ago. In part, this decline is due to persecution but losses on road and railway have been very high, too. Large numbers of animals have been killed on the roads, particularly where new motorways have been constructed. Casualties in some localities have been colossal. One reason for this is that where a traditional badger path crosses a new road, use of that route continues. Recently, in one or two places where the motorway is upon an embankment, an attempt to relieve some of the danger has been made by providing a drain or tunnel under the new road along the line of the traditional path. Of course, such provision is not always practicable, and is only possible where there is embankment, but badgers do make use of these safer routes.

This use of a tunnelled route by badgers is not entirely surprising for they rapidly learn to use badger gates. At one period before World War II the Forestry Commission appeared to be hostile to the badger, not because of its effect upon trees but due to the damage inflicted upon fencing erected to keep out rabbits. Few fences will stop a badger if they are constructed across its traditional line of route. The problem is very simply overcome by the provision of a badger gate, a flap placed in an opening in the fence at an appropriate position. Experience has shown that only badgers make use of these gates and thus live usefully in forestry plantations without providing the means for easy entrance by destructive rabbits.

The recent rather general decline in badger numbers has not been universal throughout the country. In counties with extensive woodland, like Sussex, there is a very substantial badger population, despite the urban development of so many villages and the gradual transition of many parts of the county into little more than a London suburb. Yet the physical features of the South East allow much of it to continue to be good badger territory. The Mammal Society's Survey[16] has recorded the existence of over 500 Sussex setts, well over half of them in deciduous woodland or copse.

In parts of Gloucestershire and Sussex it is probable that a population of 1:150 acres occurs and it may be even more dense in certain localities. In parts of West Yorkshire too, the population could certainly reach levels which would be regarded as abundant were it not for persecution. The end of harassment should lead to recovery and a very pleasing increase in numbers but even if this is achieved a population in excess of 1 to 300 or 400 acres is unlikely to be reached.

Setts near or within my own area of West Yorkshire provide some illustration of the general situation throughout the country. South Yorkshire's busiest setts are all within, but not far from, the edge of a wood. The three largest setts are extensive indeed, their size being the major reason for their continued occupancy despite regular visits from diggers. Adults and cubs have been killed or taken from each of these setts in recent years so that the families they contain are smaller than might be expected.

All three of these setts are quite close to motorways and other heavily used roads. However, these roads are not so near as to make traffic losses particularly heavy. I mentioned earlier the sett which is still active even though close to a motorway junction complex. It was one of twenty active setts in the area in the early 1960s. Sadly, there are less than that number of occupied setts today, persecution rather than traffic having caused the decline.

In one part of the locality the ground seems ideal for badgers but there are no active setts, although two did exist there a long time ago. The area is preserved and extensively keepered so that it is highly unlikely that diggers could have destroyed the badgers in acts of trespass. I fear that the responsibility is more likely to be that of a particularly zealous gamekeeper in the past.

Fortunately the deserted setts in South Yorkshire are near enough to active ones to allow repopulation at an early date. Also they are not in a position to engender the consequences of the strong territorial and family consciousness of the badger, a fact too often ignored when badgers are released in the wild. Many attempts at release and establishment have failed as a result of the aggressive response of the existing population. I can think of only two places in my own area where release would offer any chance of success and, if any recovery takes place within the next year or so, both would be likely to become unsuitable.

Parts of the country contain badgers descended from animals which either escaped from captivity or, more likely, were deliberately released by interested individuals following the disappearance or destruction of the previous population. Richard Fitter[7] has quoted the Rev H. A. Macpherson who, in 1892, said that all badgers in the Lake District descend from introduced animals which came from a trade advertised in a London newspaper. Apparently some of the setts occupied or established by these releases are still very active.

Sometimes the reasons for release were not entirely disinterested. Badgers were deliberately brought into parts of Scotland in the hope that they would clean fox earths since red mange had become a problem. On the north coast badgers established themselves after escape from captivity.

I doubt if the release of a male animal would be successful anywhere today. With a female, particularly if release takes place not too long before she is in season, the chances seem to be just a little better; providing the release is into an ideal situation and properly prepared, it may assist permanent reoccupation of the sett. In general I consider such attempts as desirable only if the animal concerned would otherwise have to be destroyed and even then mere 'dumping in a wood' would be a wrong and probably inhumane alternative.

For years, as in the Lake District, attempts have been made to assist wide distribution by removing badgers from one area and releasing them in another. Many of these moves have been unwise. If there is any existing population in the locality where the release takes place—and usually this is likely—the chances of successful transfer are slight. The local boar badger will undoubtedly not approve of the introduced animals and resentment will almost certainly be violently expressed. In the wild the animal in possession is usually the victor in any battle for territory so the chances of the newcomer being killed or seriously injured are very high. Badgers can and do inflict very serious injuries upon trespassing members of their species as has been described by writer and badger lover Phil Drabble.[6]

I was astonished to read a newspaper report some months ago of a badger attacking children and biting a boy's foot quite badly, for such incidents are rare and indeed I have always claimed that the badger is harmless to man. In fact the animal in question was one which had apparently been 'tamed' but then left to survive on its own. It was scarcely able to do so for it had become used to man if not to children. Just as a hand-reared owl is unlikely to be able to survive in the wild, so a badger brought up in domesticity will never be allowed to develop the skills essential for survival.

I hope that before many years have elapsed the increasing tendency to steal a march on the Jones by keeping unusual pets will have diminished. Alligators and other creatures unsuitable for the domestic environment are now on sale in pet shops. The scale of this trade and of the inevitable and swift mortality of the creatures involved has become quite excessive and a cause for concern. A reluctance to rely upon legislation and a preference for the unordered establishment of decency and common sense may be acceptable. If such values are inadequately asserted then the law must provide the relevant restraints sooner or later. At least the trade in badger cubs has now become illegal.

It is also illegal to dig badgers with the aim of attempting repopulation elsewhere, for it is now thought best to allow natural population increase to lead to occupation of setts in those areas where badgers do not exist at the present time. If the Badgers Act is effective it may take several years before marked recovery becomes clearly noticeable even in areas where persecution has been most severe. Badgers born in 1974 will not produce cubs before the winter of 1976, and the number of cubs born in Britain in 1974 is almost certain to be less than the number born five or six years earlier. Persecution since that time has markedly reduced the breeding stock, though older badgers may have survived rather more frequently than younger ones. It could be several years before numbers reach the level of a decade ago. A longer period may elapse before increased density in many localities reaches a level which leads to permanent occupation of setts in currently unpopulated districts.

The Badger Survey Recorder for Staffordshire, Maurice Waterhouse, has carried out a detailed examination of the county. His work shows that there were just over 300 setts in Staffordshire in 1973, most of them in the northern areas, and he considers that there might have been an additional 50 setts unrecorded. The bulk of the survey was carried out after 1971 so that Mr Waterhouse witnessed the severe effect of large-scale persecution. He has the names of 37 badger diggers in the county and notes that digging took place at 218 setts in the three years to 1973. Badgers may not have been taken or killed at every one of these setts but losses must have been very considerable.

While on this subject it is worth noting the harassment of several setts in the grounds of the Doncaster College of Education; the incidents can be regarded as typical. In May 1968 a sow badger was found shot at point blank range, abdominal wounds having been inflicted from a 12 bore weapon. The sett nearby had been dug and the shot badger's teeth and jaw had been broken by what seemed to be the sharp edge of a spade. Persecution continued and in October 1972 a toothed spring trap was found set in a shallow pit on a badger path near a sett. This was very close to a nature trail which was used by 3,600 children during the academic year. A local RSPCA inspector later discovered a supply of heavy duty snares, similar to ones used at other setts in the locality, hidden in the college grounds.

Mr Waterhouse also confirms that snaring was common in his area. He has recorded 35 cases of snared badgers, most of these occurring in West Staffordshire, and he notes that 32 of the snares had been placed by trespassers on private land.

Given a population of, say, 1,000 badgers, the number of litters likely to be born in one year could be estimated at about 200. Even if an average of two cubs per litter are successfully weaned this means that really no more than 400 cubs could be confidently expected.

Of the setts dug and rendered inactive in Staffordshire only 43 had been reoccupied by the autumn of 1973. Legal protection should be sufficient to maintain the population. We must remember that, in addition to digging and other persecution, there are other considerable tolls in areas like Staffordshire which contain and adjoin heavily populated districts and generate or attract heavy traffic volumes.

We can examine this question of population growth and harassment from evidence in one locality over a period of time. The following assessment is based upon observation in one territory in my own area over a six-year period.

Year One The 'family' consisted of four adults over two years of age, two yearlings and four surviving cubs of the two litters produced during the year. Towards the end of that year one of the adults was killed on the road and one cub was thought to die from accidental poisoning.

Year Two Now there were five adults of breeding age, the three animals born the previous year and five cubs from the two litters produced during the year. Then one adult disappeared or died of natural causes, one of the yearlings was killed by an irresponsible gun and a cub was killed on the road. At the end of the year there were ten animals within the territory.

Year Three Following digging in the early spring there remained five adults of breeding age, two yearlings and three cubs. Two litters had been produced but one was removed. During the year one adult died of natural causes, one of the cubs was killed on the road and another wandered out of the wood to be killed by a local man who wondered what it was. At the end of the year the family consisted of seven animals.

Year Four By the summer there were six adults, the one surviving yearling and five weaned cubs from two litters, both of the adult sows having bred. Later, one adult died of natural causes, and another adult and a cub were killed on the road whilst a second cub died in a snare set for a fox.

Year Five Now there were five adults, three yearlings and six cubs from the two litters born during the year. That summer one sett was dug, an adult being killed and two cubs removed. Another adult disappeared and one yearling was killed on the road, leaving a total of nine at the end of the year.

Year Six Five adults, four yearlings and three cubs from the one litter of the year remained. One adult and one cub died from road injuries. Ten animals were living in the territory at the end of December.

The necessarily heavily fictitious account of a family population experience may be regarded as not untypical. Despite consistent breeding success the population resulting from a total of ten animals may be no higher five or six years later. If one fairly recent statement that litters of eleven have been seen is true, a dramatic transformation could soon occur, but any suggestion that large litters are possible or could survive seems little better than nonsense.

I believe this account of badger life to be common to many areas, so that population explosions are most unlikely and increase in numbers may be achieved only slowly.

During the Committee Stage of the Badgers Bill I estimated that there are some 40–50,000 badgers in this country, perhaps 10–20,000 less than a few years ago. My figure may have been wildly inaccurate, but examination of the Mammal Society's survey[16] backs up my thinking. It shows that there are records of at least 4,300 setts in 22 counties (20 English, 1 Scottish and 1 Welsh) which I consider justifies belief that there are about 12,000 setts existing in Britain. Assuming an average occupation of three badgers per sett there would be a population of 36,000.

Whilst some of the well populated counties were surveyed by the Mammal Society one or two counties which are likely to show a great number of setts, such as Gloucestershire and Devon, were not included. I should be surprised if these two counties did not contain many more than 1,000 setts each. With the addition of other areas not yet surveyed and, bearing in mind the likelihood that more setts may exist than the individual recorders may know of, then a figure of more than 12,000 setts is possible. This would seem to me to provide a population less, but not very much less, than my 'off the cuff' estimate of 40–50,000.

If I were to revise the figure I would put the present badger population at 35,000. I believe that if we have that number now then the position in 1968 would have showed at least 45,000 and possibly 50,000 animals—probably twice as many as at the beginning of the century. The justification for protection then seems well established.

If such estimates have any accuracy then it is possible to offer some assessment of recent population changes and likely further change. January 1969 might have seen a population of 45,000, 13,000 of these being the survivors of the cubs born the previous year. Of the adults at least 10,000 sows could be expected to have been in cub and 26,000 cubs might have been born during the year. Probably little more than half the cubs born would be alive by the end of the year with a loss during that time of 12,000 adults and yearlings. The population at the end of 1969 could well have been 13,000 cubs and 33,000 older animals.

It was 1970 that saw an increase in persecution. Perhaps 25,000 cubs may again have been born but it is possible that no more than 10,000 were alive at the end of the year, whilst 9,000 adults and 5,000 yearlings might have died or been killed over the period. Total population would then fall to 42,000.

In 1971, say 24,000 cubs were born but with digging activity increasing steadily only 10,000 of these probably survived at the end of the year and 9,000 adults and 4,000 yearlings might also have been lost. The population could well have fallen to below 40,000 with mortality higher among younger animals.

The result was that in 1972 no more than 8,000 cubs, 6,000

yearlings and 23,000 adults were alive at the year end, a population of 35,000. In a number of areas persecution clearly began to decline in 1973 and, despite the fall in the number of litters, a population of 10,000 cubs might well have survived at the end of the year together with about 5,000 yearlings and 20,000 older animals. This figure would seem to have held steady throughout 1974, even increasing somewhat.

The decline in population can thus be assumed to have ceased except in a few districts. Yet population growth is unlikely to be noticeable for some time. My estimate of the position in the next few years is presented in the following table.

	Adults	Yearlings	Cubs	Total
January 1975	26,000	10,000	18,000 (due)	
losses	6,000	3,000	7,000	
December 1975	20,000	7,000	11,000	37,000
January 1976	27,000	11,000	19,000 (due)	
losses	6,000	3,000	7,000	
December 1976	21,000	8,000	12,000	41,000
January 1977	29,000	12,000	20,000 (due)	
losses	7,000	4,000	7,000	
December 1977	22,000	8,000	13,000	43,000
January 1978	30,000	12,000	21,000 (due)	
losses	7,000	4,000	7,000	
December 1978	23,000	8,000	14,000	45,000
January 1979	31,000	14,000	21,000 (due)	
losses	7,000	4,000	8,000	
December 1979	24,000	10,000	13,000	47,000

Provided these estimates are correct then, nationally, numbers cannot increase in any dramatic way. It may well take the rest of the decade before we return to the population position we assume applied in the late 1960s.

CHAPTER 7

AN ANCIENT BRITON:
The Badger in Myth, History and Literature

The badger's residence in Britain goes back before the dawn of human consciousness. Certainly it is known to have lived here before the Neolithic period, if not before, and cannot be regarded as other than indigenous in these islands. Even in those areas of Britain that today contain no setts it may be possible to identify an earlier population from local place-names. If no settlement is linked to the badger by name it may be possible to recognise an association from the name given to a local farm, field, wood or even a lane, although a Brock Avenue on a post-war housing estate can obviously be attributable only to the fact that the badger is now accepted as a respectable species!

Older place-names linked with the badger abound. The derivation may not be from the one word badger for that was only one of the names given to the species. Others are 'brock', 'grey', 'pate' and 'bawson' depending on a regional basis.

Brock has an ancient origin in that the Danish and the Gaelic name for the species is 'broc', whilst bawson is also an ancient word devolving from Scandinavian, meaning striped with white. 'Grey' was commonly applied in much of medieval England and 'pate' seems to have been fairly common in the North, certainly in the Lake District and in parts of the North East. Gradually, by the eighteenth century, the name badger had become generally accepted although regional preferences were still maintained by villagers. Badger itself appears related to 'becheur', a French name for the animal which means digger.

Most of these various names for the species can be found in British place-names, such as: Altnambroc (Ross-shire); Carn-broc (Ayrshire); Craignambroc (Argyllshire); Monabroc (Ren-frewshire); Brockdam (Dorset); Brockenhurst (Hampshire); Brockhall (Northamptonshire); Brockham (Surrey); Brock-hampton (Gloucestershire); Brockholes (Yorkshire, West Riding); Brocklesby (Lincolnshire, Lindsey); Brockley (Somerset); Brockley Green (Suffolk); Brocton (Staffordshire); Badger (Shropshire); Badger's Mount (Kent); Grays Wood (Surrey); Pateley Bridge (Yorkshire, West Riding).

Despite the obvious recognition of the animal shown by the existence of so many place-names there was also a great deal of ignorance about the species. The inevitable contact with nature springing from the rural character of Britain in the past seems not to have provided any clear knowledge and understanding. Indeed, in some places the ill-informed assumptions of the Middle Ages and after still seem to exist.

In view of the lack of protein in the diet of many ordinary people centuries ago, it may well have been fortunate that the level of superstition in the villages seems to have been quite high, otherwise the practice of digging and taking badgers might have been more frequent.

Yet badgers were undoubtedly eaten as shown by Vyner's comment that their hams should be 'smoked and grated like tongue or dried beef which they far excel in flavour'.

He added that he could 'answer for their excellence'.[33] And in 1914 Sir Alfred Pease and Mr J. F. Blakeborough noted that a party of gipsies said that they preferred badger to hedgehog although it was hard to skin an old badger.[25] Indeed a few hotels and restaurants had badger ham on their menus as recently as 1973 and I am informed that diggers were offered £5 for a pair of badger hams in Stoke on Trent.

Many people today still feel that woodland is best avoided after dark. This irrational fear may be responsible for the badger's being linked with primitive fancies and legends. Ours was a land of superstition until quite recent years. Potions of alleged magic propensity were often in demand and, to be effective, some charms needed to contain badger blood. One charm demanded that seven drops of this blood had to be mixed with part of the skull taken from the body of a man who had been hanged upon a gibbet, the mixture having to be made seven years from the day that the malefactor was hanged. It was also believed that if a bone or a claw of a badger were hung from the neck then the wearer would have the power to keep a secret.[25]

For much of the eighteenth century those with literary inclination were more attracted by urban fashion and activity than by the country. The peasantry at that time were largely illiterate, generally immobile and frequently given to superstitious fancy. It is hardly surprising then that the badger's nocturnal habits contributed to its being linked with the superstitions of the times.

The badger may have received protective benefit from an unwitting capacity to cause terror as a result of the old belief which said that to hear a badger's cry followed by an owl's betokened death. To my knowledge, there is no record of anyone entering upon an induced decline following such an experience. If such a decline had set in, recovery might have been achieved by taking the advice of a Mistress Braithwaite, who was quoted by Blakeborough as saying that good fortune would follow if a badger crossed one's path and that 'a tuft of hair gotten from the head of a full-grown Brock is powerful to ward off all manner of witchcraft'. It was suggested that the tuft of hair was best placed in a little bag made of the skin of a black cat and worn round the neck when 'the moon was not more than a week old and Jupiter was mid-heaven at midnight'.[25]

A cure for ailments of the bladder was said to be provided by pills made from the gall of a living adult badger mixed with hare's blood, flour, dill seeds and wormwood. And a 'Clever Nanny' made a salve from badger's fat which at one time was in great request over the counties of Stirling and Perth as it was felt to be useful for treating 'burns, scalds and indeed for all sorts of hurts and wounds'.[1]

Another recipe of those times suggested that three drops of badger's blood taken at night whilst kneeling upon a grave would be efficacious if the following lines were recited:

> 'This salve I pray
> For good or ill
> May work my will
> So as I say Amen.'

The best known of all the sovereign remedies obtained from badgers was published in 1800: 'The flesh, blood and grease of the badger are very useful for oils, ointments, salves and powders.' These were said to cure 'shortness of breath, the cough of the lungs, for the stone, sprained sinews, coll achs etc'. In addition a well-dressed badger skin was said to be 'very warm and comfortable for ancient people who are troubled with paralytic disorders'.[28]

Possible benefit from badger products was not restricted to man. It was thought that a horse suffering from 'greasy shank' would be cured if it stepped upon a badger's spoor.

Ignorance may have been extensive but shrewd common sense was also encountered as shown in the old north-country saying that 'a wise lass is always abed when the badger goes courting'. Despite an apparent lack of knowledge there seems to have been not only some awe for the nocturnal habits of the badger but also a rather contradictory acceptance of the badger as the undevious and rather respectable creature presented in the thirteenth-century *History of Reynard the Fox*. Perhaps this is revealed by the old saying referring to those who minded their own business being 'as close or as shy as a badger'.

For a long time it was thought that the badger's legs were shorter on one side than the other. Nicholas Cox, in his day presumably regarded as knowledgeable about these matters, wrote of the badger in 1677: 'He hath very sharp teeth and therefore is accounted a deep-biting beast; his back is broad and his legs are longer on the right side rather than the left and therefore he runneth best when he gets on the side of a Hill.' Cox added that the badger 'fights on his back with teeth and nails and by blowing up skin' in a 'strange and wonderful manner'.[5] Similarly, Macaulay referred to Titus Oates as being 'uneven as a badger'.

Whilst no one can say the badger is a particularly slow mover, its speed is not such that some unusual characteristic had to be invented for explanation. The comment about the inflation of the skin was obviously a result of inaccurate observation for the badger's coat is likely to stand out as hairs are erectile especially during periods of emotional stress. And there is even less justification for the suggestion that sett cleaning is achieved by one badger pulling another which lies upon its back whilst holding a large bundle of bedding.

Inaccurate understanding continued for many years even among those whom we might have expected to have been more knowledgeable. Nimrod for example in *The Life of a Sportsman* attributed the badger's burrowing power to the strength of its nose. He described the badger a little more fittingly as 'neither a depredator nor a thief' considering that in woods it consumed 'anything that pigs eat'.[20]

There were several errors too in the first volume devoted to the species, a monograph by a former Member of Parliament, Sir Alfred Pease,[24] published in 1898. Some of these were corrected in a new volume published sixteen years later in collaboration with Mr J. F. Blakeborough. At first Sir Alfred

Page 107 (*above*) Kim, a domesticated young sow. Making pets of badgers is inadvisable; (*below*) a mature male sets out on a nocturnal expedition

Page 108 (*top*) A family outing to a nearby garden. Away from the sett badgers often exhibit remarkable fearlessness; (*bottom*) badger covered in mud from excavating

believed that the badger was a member of the bear family. He also considered that the scent glands actually produced a substance designed to promote health, a view apparently shared by the Frenchman M Edmond le Masson whom Pease quoted as describing an incident in which a badger was walled in a culvert from 18 February to 4 April 1853: when it died the badger weighed 19lb. It was believed that in this case, and in a similar one in England where a badger is said to have survived for 44 days, subsistence was somehow provided from the secretion obtained when the animals licked their vents.

Pease did not subscribe to the hibernation theory and appreciated that the badger's gestation was abnormal. He supposed that the gestation period was normally of nine weeks length but considered that the badger, like the roe, was capable of postponing parturition for long periods.

Pease considered that the badger 'may linger on for years yet in the more secluded corners of England and Wales', but he thought the species was well-nigh extinct in Scotland. He attributed decline almost entirely to the 'intelligent and unprejudiced wearer of velveteen who with the tacit consent of their masters have by means of the steel trap, flag-trap and gun exterminated and banished for ever the most interesting of our animals and the most beautiful of our birds'.

Despite the pessimism revealed by Pease it seems clear from the information provided in the volumes of *The Victoria County History* published in the first years of the present century that in various districts there was still a substantial badger population. Obviously people like Pease, sympathetic though they were to hunting, were beginning to feel some revulsion at the rejection of natural balance which very extensive game preservation implied. As a digger Pease, as others before him and since, subscribed to the view that the hunting of a species was a way of ensuring its survival. Whilst this view can be substantiated to some extent it is impossible to accept it absolutely.

Badger digging as a sport rather than a destructive measure has also been carried out throughout this century. In 1931 Mr

H. King claimed that the badgers he dug were killed only if this were requested by the land-owner concerned.[15] He believed that the best method of destruction was to shoot at the end of a dig when the badger's face could be seen in the excavation, and felt that this method of control was more humane than the use of trap or poison.

Others, like King, made the point that badger digging as they practised it did not guarantee the certain destruction of badgers. Often the digging was unsuccessful even after a day's hard labour. When the quarry was cornered the end often took the form of the bloodless capture of a badger which was released later.

King did not believe that a dig should extend into a second day but not all exponents shared this view. In 1890 one dig in Hertfordshire is said to have lasted for ten days: eight diggers were involved but in the end no badger was caught. M le Masson also described one event when relays of workers were employed for three days and nights. And J. G. Millais refers to a Cheshire sett where a badger was killed only after digging had extended to 40ft during two days' activity.[17]

Several attempts at badger hunting by scent have been recorded. Amongst these was a Yorkshire pack of hounds from the Axe Vale. Hunting, obviously by night, the Master and the whippers-in carried lanterns on their belts. During the spring of 1902 7 adult badgers were killed and 2 got to ground.[3] Other attempts were made in the Cotswolds in 1912 when, in August, 22 badgers were found and 11 bagged. And Mortimer Batten described similar activity in North Yorkshire after that date.[2]

Such an activity is scarcely likely to be tolerated today. One suspects that even then it was largely an activity of madcaps uncaring for majority disapproval. The holes were bagged or blocked, the aim being to catch the animal before it returned to its sett and could tear its way through the obstruction to reach security.

Similar in approach, but with different intention, was the more recent action of Sir Peter Scott, who captured a badger one afternoon by racing it to the hole and throwing his umbrella over the entrance so that the cub ran into it—possibly the first and last badger to be caught by an umbrella.

In general then, throughout recorded history, although some attempts were made to preserve or re-introduce badgers to parts of the country where they were fast becoming extinct, most records speak only of animals killed and taken rather than observed. In Hertfordshire, where the last pine marten was recorded as having been killed in Oxley Wood, Watford in 1872, the badger was already becoming rare. The four records of badgers in Norfolk in the late nineteenth century noted by T. Southwell were each incidents of destruction. Two badgers were shot in 1893, one at Holkham and the other at Whittingham, whilst in 1895 a sow with two cubs was trapped at West Wretham and in 1899 an 'old sow with three cubs' was killed at Forncett.[27]

There are many other mentions of badgers being taken throughout the United Kingdom but it is always dangerous to rely upon isolated records from which to draw general assumptions. Pease, for example, considered that the badger was extinct in Durham in 1898 but, in 1905, E. L. Gill believed badgers to be plentiful in the west and also in the quieter woods in the east of the country. He noted that in the eighteenth century a refugee French priest came to County Durham and lived as a hermit.[9] Much given to badger-hunting, the priest gave his name, and that of his favourite sport, to the glen where he stayed—Pate Priest's Dene.

Cumberland parish records mention Penrith where two shillings was 'payed for the killing of two paytes' in 1658. And, in the parish of Dacre alone 36 'paytes' were killed between 1685 and 1750. The rate of this bounty was one shilling for an adult and fourpence for a cub, quite a substantial amount, sufficient to ensure that the badger population remained small at best. This practice of payment from parish funds for the destruction of predators were quite widespread and may have been an important factor in controlling numbers in the years before game preservation exercised a markedly severe influence upon the predatory species.

Badger baiting was a popular form of entertainment, being one of the activities offered at the annual Sandridge Fair near St Albans, as well as more unorthodox events organised by publicans throughout the country.

Ill-founded but long-standing attitudes may best be illustrated by an advertisement, published in 1911 which read: 'Extraordinary capture at Stainton near Darlington of a Monster Badger which terrified the district with its destruction of sheep and cattle.' It was claimed that the badger was captured only after a desperate fight. In fact, the animal turned out to be half-grown and fed only on fish although it was said to have looked well. This badger was advertised as an exhibit at Wensleydale's annual Leyburn Fair, and was meant as an attraction for country folk.[2] Fletcher's assumption of rural ignorance does sometimes seem to have been justified!

This use of badgers as a spectacle was not only a rural pastime for they were also taken to towns to provide sport as at Colinton in 1880 when badger baiting was arranged to entertain the officers based in Edinburgh Castle.[1] Apparently a disagreeable impression was created for 'Brock had to be smoked before he would leave his earth'. The badger was then seized by the dog at the entrance and 'a terrific and bloody struggle' ensued. The dog 'speedily had the worst' and a fresh dog also 'speedily succumbed'.

Indeed baiting seems to have been common in the Edinburgh area. On one occasion two badgers fought and killed three dogs on the estate of a Mr Inglis on the banks of the Leith, then escaped. On another, in baiting organised by a Mr Ramsay to entertain his visiting Stirlingshire tenants, the badger killed three dogs before it was 'bottled up for another day'.[1]

In some districts, by the middle of the last century, baiting, the tormenting or fighting of a captive or chained animal, had given way to arrangements for more direct fighting. *The Malton Messenger* printed an account of a 'fight' between a badger weighing 22lb and a 'Manchester' terrier of 18lb which lasted half an hour before the badger died.[2]

Over a century later, as man progressed in knowledge and understanding of the need to conserve dying species of wildlife, it would be not unnatural to imagine that some ancient cruelties would ebb away and that badger digging for entertainment would cease. Unfortunately, the practice increased extensively during the last decade and in 1972 it was carried out in thirty counties in England and Wales. In that year I personally visited two setts which had been vandalised by diggers. Square pits had been very neatly excavated to considerable depths near the setts, which were clearly not part of the extraction operations. A little earlier, near one of these setts a badger was found which had suffered severe injuries.

I do not suggest that all those who have practised badger digging for sport in recent years are guilty of even more revolting practices, but it is clear that these have frequently taken place as proved by witnessed accounts and photographs. One item of evidence produced by the Mammal Society's County Recorders during the legislation for the Badgers Bill was a photograph taken only a little while before, showing a chained badger being attacked by nine dogs.

Earlier writers like Pease and King appear to have regarded the badger they dug with affection and only killed if requested. Unfortunately, in recent years most digging seems to have been of rather more barbaric purpose. In many areas the greater incidence of digging has taken place in the spring when cubs are small, and no doubt many of these have been sold as pets.

The badger might be fascinating but it is not a domestic animal nor is it really suitable for household living. Some of those who have taken cubs either as a novel play-thing or, for the worthier reason of not wishing to see them die, have learned of their eventual domestic unsuitability. Badger's jaws are extremely strong and play can be unintentionally painful. Their inquisitiveness is tremendous and their wit sufficient to satisfy curiosity sometimes with quite devastating results. I suppose that if there is time to allow the badger a natural routine, to sleep through much of the day and to be able to provide companionable play during every evening before allowing nocturnal freedom then a satisfactory *modus vivendi* could be established. But evidence suggests that on the whole urban existence for the badger is not at all suitable and once the novelty has worn off domestication is likely to become a serious and demanding chore.

Through the years badgers have been domesticated on many occasions. Pease himself took cubs as pets, whilst A. H. Cocks, who described the position of the species in Buckinghamshire in 1905, claimed to have kept many badgers. Cocks noted cases where captive badgers had lived for over fifteen years and he had to have one destroyed at the age of fourteen. One test of successful captivity is whether the animals breed successfully. A Mr F. H. Salvin of Guildford was said to have bred and reared badgers in captivity in the latter part of last century.[4] And a more unusual piece of evidence of happy domesticity occurred in the early years of this century when *The Field* reported that a badger regularly accompanied its owner, a Mr Burge of Northleach, when he rode his bicycle.

Much of the information passed on about the species in past years appears to have been based upon experience of captive badgers. Yet captivity might well be a cause of untypical or unnatural behaviour so such evidence might well be regarded with hesitation. Indeed, information offered by those who have kept captive badgers seems often to be contradictory. Often a case has been stated in absolute terms as when J. E. Harting categorically claimed that he could settle the question of gestation. He stated that his sow mated on 27 February 1886 and produced cubs on 16 February 1887 so that gestation lasted 'one year all but seventeen days'.[11] On the contrary, evidence of captive badgers from J. Paterson of Rutherford suggested that the duration of gestation was seven months.[22]

Similarly there is conflicting evidence about the age at which cubs' eyes are open. A. H. Cocks said that a captive litter in his collection remained blind for thirty days although he qualified this by admitting that the badger's box was too dark to admit of certain observation.[4] Paterson however claimed that cubs were blind for six weeks. I rather think it is for a shorter time than that although, of course, eyes are of remarkably little use until evening emergence commences several weeks later.

Nor has our knowledge of badgers been increased by references in literature. Somewhat surprisingly, for such an ancient animal, our classics contain few mentions of the badger, even as an object of sport. Proof of the age-old use of the skin as a furnishing is given in *The Bible* when describing the Temple, but this can hardly be claimed as pertaining to the British badger in particular.

Strangely too perhaps there have been few poems about the species, including John Clare's *Badger*, Patrick Chalmers's *A Peck o' Mant* and Eden Phillpotts's *The Badgers*. It is tempting to speculate on the possible absence of badgers in the Lake District when Wordsworth was writing . . .

Possibly some of the most penetrating stories about badgers written this century are Henry Williamson's *The Badger Dig* and *The Epic of Brock the Badger*, the first of which presents a rather controlled but piercing analysis of a dig and those involved in it. The story of Brock, written in the style of the author's more famous *Tarka the Otter*, reveals both understanding and concern, for Williamson approached the badger with sympathy if without an entirely accurate knowledge. Unfortunately the comments concerning his badger-hero's diet may not have been wholly advantageous to the species for his Brock is supposed to have taken sucking pigs, one on each of five consecutive nights. The badger was also so stubbornly courageous as to have left his sett to attack a full pack of hounds!

Such attractive representations of the badger can only have done good in getting rid of prejudice and furthering our understanding of the species. The badger has been an object of suspicion and superstition for centuries, regarded as a mysterious creature of the night, with magical propensities, viewed with an unjustified animosity by those with agricultural and sporting interests and all too often killed on sight. Fortunately more and more individual land-owners, farmers and estate managers have recently adopted the view of those few individuals who offered protection before this century began. Attitudes have changed greatly. Increased esteem has made legislation possible and the Badgers Act should assist or secure extensive survival whilst it will not prevent proper observation. Accurate and sensibly conducted observation is necessary for, as I think I have made clear, we still have much to learn about this ancient species.

CHAPTER 8

WATCHING BADGERS

I suppose that in the last ten years I have seen more than 200 different badgers, but on only half-a-dozen occasions has a sighting been entirely unexpected and unplanned. It is possible to go for years without any undesigned encounter so, for anyone wishing to see a badger prior arrangement is necessary.

Since a badger uses its paths regularly then, ideally, observation by a well-trodden route should be rewarded, yet even if the badger does use the chosen path it may not do so until it has been dark for hours, and in the dark—and frequently cold—conditions no proper view of the animal can be enjoyed. With good fortune the view might still be very fleeting indeed. Taking up a position at or near the sett is the only way likely to offer a good chance of fruitful observation. Endeavour to watch and depart without disturbance and, therefore, without immediate detection, a situation which is not always possible.

It is wise to visit the selected sett during the day to ascertain its layout and plan the best approach; a daylight visit will allow a particular hole to be noted for evening observation. Such selection may be essential at a large sett on uneven ground with much vegetation. At some setts the hole of emergence may be obvious from evidence of use or lack of other open entrances, although such a situation is very infrequently found. Several open holes are usually noticeable with the most well-trodden exits or entrances being obvious. The hole to watch is not necessary one into which bedding is taken for, at many setts, bedding may be taken into a different hole from the one used for emergence. This practice is sensible, for sometimes the quantity of bedding being taken into or out of the sett is so substantial that it might impede rapid escape.

If there are many holes visible look for one which is clearly open and obviously well used. Sometimes it is possible to assess the use of the hole from the footmarks. You can often distinguish the marks of the long claws which are to be seen in a direct line from the pads and direction may be thus ascertained. The badger's footmark is clearly distinguishable, of course, from the half-round smaller print of the neatly-footed fox. Usually however, holes are so much used that no clear footprint can exist, although it is always advisable to look for one before the time chosen for observation. But do not tramp round the sett on a prior visit several weeks before the selected evening, or even an hour or two before the watch is to commence. In the first case such a visit would be premature for patterns of activity can change; in the second the disturbance might inhibit activity that evening.

If a choice of entrance or exits still remains then it would be as well to select that hole which is furthest from the path of the prevailing wind, which may be best and most quietly approached. On a preliminary visit to a sett note the likely wind direction so as to work out that line of route to the sett which will be into the wind and through sufficiently thin vegetation, allowing as noiseless an approach as possible. Bear in mind also that some setts are almost unwatchable in the late summer months because of these natural conditions.

If the approach can be silent and into the wind it will not be necessary to arrive hours before emergence can be expected. A long wait in a wood can be of great discomfort particularly if insects are biting and stillness has to be maintained. In such a situation a shorter wait may be well worth a more cautious approach. Otherwise the observer might feel driven to depart before any sign of a badger could be detected.

In the summer the watcher may be quite unable to avoid some movement for the attention of midge and mosquito can be almost intolerable. The use of insect repellent may be effective although I suspect that the type which I last used, and which is quite effective, provides a smell which is particularly detectable.

The best way of reducing the opportunity offered to insect marauders is by ensuring that target areas are reduced. Providing the minimum area of exposed or thinly covered skin and particularly ensuring that hands and ankles are well protected may be worth while and sufficient protection. In addition, a steady approach to the sett in a manner not conducive to perspiration might be wise.

In winter too, suitable clothing is essential as is a strong torch, and even a small compass. On one December evening's observation a fairly strong south-westerly wind blew and I went deep into the wood in order to approach the sett from the best angle. This wood is thick, the part of it where I was heading is not regularly visited and it is a long time since there was forestry work. When I was a good way into the wood my torch faded and finally died, leaving me deep in a part of a dense wood with which I was not at all familiar. I groped my way in the darkness and reached a large yew in a little clearing before striking out in the direction I thought appropriate. This choice was not assisted by a moderation in the wind's intensity, nor by the fact that I could not detect any useful star in the bits of sky which were unclouded or visible through the trees. Fifteen minutes later I found myself back by the large yew in a little clearing and it began to rain.

Even our own kindly lowland nature should not be treated

with disdain. My experience emphasises the need for a torch with a non-senile battery at night in any woodland with which one is unfamiliar. My thornproof, waterproof jacket also proved its worth that night for it received and withstood both rough use and heavy wetting before I returned home.

During a preliminary visit it might be as well to select the point of watchfulness. As previously mentioned this should be a tree or some other substantial object to avoid any sharp break in the existing visual pattern. A position upon smooth ground providing an even and silent footing is also to be recommended. Often, of course, there may be a conveniently placed stout branch above ground. I hesitate to recommend this, for a branch may soon become a most uncomfortable seat and it may not always be secure. I once sat upon a quite wide branch, fortunately only a couple of feet or so off the ground, which snapped just as a badger emerged. He departed promptly and I saw no other animal that night! Also a branch may not allow easy movement and if it is high a descent in darkness may not be wise. Normally, I prefer to lean against a tree although at one sett I sit upon a conveniently placed log. Having taken up position all that remains is to wait quietly and there can be no absolute guarantee as to how long that wait may need to be.

Sometimes, of course, a vigil is fruitless and the reason cannot be readily explained. Perhaps a fickleness of the wind took scent to a badger's nose as it waited a foot or two inside the sett. Badgers do often wait not far from the entrance for an unconscionable time. I once watched a boar standing perfectly still at the bend of the passage leading to the entrance with only the tip of its nose visible. It stood there for twenty minutes and only the long light of a mid-summer evening allowed the detection. So, before emergence and sighting, a period of silence and an absence of the circumstances of betrayal are essential.

Several reasons may cause the watcher to be disappointed such as a wind change, other persons passing nearby both noisy and unexpected, or that day there may have been serious disturbance. My wife and I once watched at a large sett for several hours and saw no badger. Later we learned that the family had departed the night before and temporarily taken up quarters in another, smaller sett not far away, following attempted persecution. There is usually a sound reason for such non-appearances.

Three of my disappointments stand out. One was when I visited a South Yorkshire sett for the second evening in succession. On the previous night I had seen a fox emerge from the sett to be followed fifteen minutes later by three badgers. They had come from a hole I had not expected to be used and the fox from another hole only two or three yards away—from the relative absence of odour it was not its permanent abode. The next evening I reached the wood just before 7.30 pm and this time I had my camera ready. I found a suitable position and waited. No badgers appeared. A few days later I noticed that there were four badgers at this sett. I can only conclude that since I had made little sound, and since I am sure that I was not betrayed by the wind, the fourth badger had discerned my presence on the first of the two evenings and in some way counselled that caution which caused my disappointment.

Some years earlier I visited one sett regularly over a period of six or seven weeks. I noted the pattern of activity and on several evenings arrived just before the animals emerged. On five consecutive visits my presence behind a tree only eight or ten feet away went unnoticed at the time. My scent must have been detected afterwards, of course, but my close proximity seemed to be immediately unremarked. Then, the next two evenings I was soon noticed and left almost immediately to ensure that cause for suspicion or particular wariness was minimised. On the next visit to that sett, two or three days later, suspicion was marked and only a brief testing of the air was observed. Yet two days later confidence was replaced with the cubs romping as happily as before, and they indeed came so close that one backed into my ankle without undue alarm. So do not be deterred by one or two disappointing experiences.

Another time I arrived at a wood very early to find only a

short distance from the sett—and not very far from a woodcock's nest—a happy family picnic. Obviously the young people were entitled to indulge their taste for pop music, and my feelings may have been unjustifiably uncharitable at the din coming from a transistor radio hanging from the branch of a tree. Naturally I saw no badgers that night. Yet I suppose that I was fortunate in arriving when I did, otherwise the family might have departed before I had heard them and would not have realised why the badgers were reluctant to emerge that evening.

Where peace has long been established, whilst some suspicion is natural, observation is likely to be easier and at such setts photography can be possible and not unduly alarming. In such cases a single flash might cause no more than a momentary interruption of play, but it seems to me to be rather pointless for an observer to regularly cart around the paraphernalia of photography. Photographic apparatus, even if handled in silence, requires a certain amount of movement and, although the badger's sight is not acute, observation may still be inhibited by either the movement or the detectable sound which accompanies activity.

There can be no taking of nature for granted. If the sett is disturbed and if there has been serious cause for caution then it may well take a long time for the badgers occupying the sett concerned to settle down into a routine of only normal vigilance. This question of disturbance by watchers is not one which can be dismissed lightly. As interest in natural history increases so some setts near, and accessible to, urban areas may be visited too often to permit the badgers' normal patterns of behaviour to be maintained. Although the coldness of winter nights provides an annual breathing space it is hardly helpful if enthusiasts frequent a sett every summer evening, particularly if there is a family of cubs. It may be a useful lesson for them to be alarmed occasionally but nightly interruption or prevention of play is hardly likely to be beneficial.

At some setts it is possible that within a few years we could reach a position in which human observers will be in attendance by a sett on more evenings than not between April and October. For this reason increases in population and in the number of setts seem desirable if only to provide enthusiasts with less concentrated and inhibiting opportunity. For the same reason, too, disturbance of setts by watchers should be avoided and silent stillness maintained as far as possible.

Some might be tempted to render apology by taking food for the badgers. I must confess that I have fed wild badgers myself but a regular practice is best avoided since it cannot generally be maintained and, therefore, inculcation of habit and reliance is to be deplored. In most circumstances the badger can manage perfectly well on the natural fare it is able to obtain for itself.

It is also quite probable that regular feeding may not benefit all the animals at one sett. It may well be that only one or two of the badgers will accept the offering; possibly the dominant boar may decide to take all for himself and the others in the family may refrain from encroaching upon what he regards as his privilege.

Another disadvantage of feeding is that it may encourage excessive tameness which is hardly desirable in areas where the badger might be in danger. Of course, many badgers do forage around homes and farms although not, I think, to the same extent as foxes. Evidence of badger visitation, though, is likely to be more emphatic for the fox is much more lightly footed and less likely to dig holes in lawns or flower beds. Badgers can be a nuisance if these activities become habitual. Preventive measures can be taken which may reduce the likelihood of damage. These include laying a scent trail of creosote or napthalene across their path of entry or hanging material impregnated with a repellent substance across the path 6in above the ground. Bottles of ammonia, buried to neck level at the point of entry, might also be a temporary preventative. Fencing unless very expensively and solidly constructed will not prevent access. Many of those who are visited by badgers welcome them for not everyone can boast of such attractive features in their gardens. In most cases the visitors may do remarkably little damage, although I must admit that there are less happy examples, like the MP who lost almost all of the scores of bulbs planted in his garden to badgers!

Generally we do not need to encourage unnatural habits and on the whole badgers need to live in as wild a manner as possible, adapting to the changing environment certainly, but not becoming mere semi-domestics. A self-denying ordinance upon amateur naturalists against too frequent and disturbing visitation and regular feeding might be desirable.

For the truly objective observer who takes precautions, is silent and does not disturb the badgers' pattern of life, rewards are enormous. One September evening, for example, I noted in detail my experiences. I parked by the roadside approximately 300yd from the sett. As there was a south-westerly breeze of barely moderate strength on reaching the wood I kept to the eastern side and walked about 60yd to the north of the sett before turning to approach it into the wind. I walked slowly to the occupied sett so that I could stand by a tree three or four yards from, and directly before, the north-facing main exit from which badgers had appeared a couple nights earlier.

Unfortunately, my appearance coincided with a badger's early emergence and we appeared to notice each other simultaneously. The badger, an adult boar of mature years, promptly turned back. I saw him when I was only six or seven yards away, so perhaps pointlessly I walked a few more steps towards the sett, then noticeably retraced my steps and walked a little distance away. After about ten minutes I moved back towards the sett as quietly as I could and leaned against a tree to await another appearance. As I waited I heard a woodpigeon coming into roost in a birch tree nearby. Then came the first of the night's noises from one of a pair of tawny owls which had taken up residence in the wood that year.

Fifteen minutes later the woodcock came over. I am always pleased to see woodcock fly above the sett for it often seems to support a pet theory of mine. Time after time, within three or four minutes of the birds' roding badgers have emerged, and I like to think that somehow the woodcock acts as a 'morning call' for the badger. This is obviously coincidental but on that night a badger appeared at the sett five minutes after the woodcock flew overhead.

The face alone was in sight for six minutes, just the head, level with the entrance, moving slightly in suspicious care. Then the badger, a boar, stepped slowly out to stand for a minute a foot away from the hole. Another badger was immediately behind him. This one came out and moved further away as the boar sniffed about close by, the head and neck in sinewy, seemingly elastic, movement. A third badger appeared then moved back into the sett. For a moment I thought that it had somehow detected me. All was well, for there was prompt emergence of the third and a fourth badger from another hole to my right. This hole is higher, above the little slope and at the side of a large tree.

The two badgers by this tree began grooming, one rubbing against the selected tree the other apparently scratching its front and sides in that most comical of all badger positions when it appears to balance on the lower middle of its back as if seated upon an ill-designed chair. I watched this activity for ten minutes before one of the sows walked in my direction until she almost touched me. Then she caught my scent. There was a slight but breath-expelling grunt of surprise and all four animals shot below.

Another sett was visited in December. The night was cold but dry with the moon almost full. The ground had recently been churned by a tractor but it was not frozen and the footing was hard which frequently led to the crunching of ice and earth beneath my feet. A rather noisy approach to the sett was unavoidable and when I reached it all was quiet and still. The crisp air seemed undisturbed by wind and there was no sign of motion. Then I caught a sound at one of the holes. This hole, a comparatively new one, was at the base of a wide, decades-old ridge of badger-displaced earth now grown over. However, it was unusual in that the area immediately inside the hole appeared to be in use as a chamber, for I felt flattened and dry bedding within inches of the opening itself and this seemed to be warm. The slight noise I heard may have been made by the badger retreating to a secure chamber further into the depths of this large sett.

A fortnight later the bedding was still there in this very unusual position so near the surface. I can only presume that the badger feels confident in that the situation is certainly not an insecure one. Silent approach is almost impossible and the opening is well sited to catch scent and sound. In addition it is relatively central to the sett so that early warning is very likely to be received.

My observations of badgers and nature in general make me believe that Richard Jefferies had it right. He may not have enjoyed much contact with badgers but some of his beliefs seem to me to be of increasing relevance. 'Mechanism increases convenience—in no way does it confer physical or moral perfection.'[13] We need at least half a wilderness. Natural contact for many people is seen as a desirable part of their existence. It allows them, again using Jefferies's words, to 'get away from the endless and nameless circumstances of everyday existence which by degrees build a wall about the mind so that it travels in a constantly narrowing circle'.

I suppose that this is one reason why I enjoy getting off the London train in Yorkshire at the end of each week. I have adapted to urban existence but that adaptation cannot be entirely complete. Occasionally I greatly value a darkening wood, the evening in a degree of isolation, with the sound of birds, the breeze and the uneven recession of light. Such moments in the dusk may seem sombre, but as the wealth of light fades so sound seems nearer and scent a little more acute. At such a time the intensity of light may be restricted but it has not ebbed completely.

Artists may present such scenes, and their painting may create more than a photographic representation, but the increase of shade and shadow, the growing imperception of sight, is only part of the content of the observer's evening. Painting may convey little of the day's dying, of the noise in the wood or of the scent of the dusk; nor can art exactly present so clearly as reality the cool touch of the breeze and all the other noticeable sensations of natural existence. In these moments of broadened awareness it seems fitting that such a quietly impressive animal as the badger should appear. I hope that it will continue to add a unique distinction to our evenings.

CHAPTER 9

BROCK TRIUMPHANT?

It is clear that so far the vast economic and social changes which have occurred in Great Britain have not been entirely destructive of the badger and that in many ways the species has proved to be adaptable. I have already discussed the possibility that in previous centuries the badger may not have been so abundant as might be assumed in view of the nature of pre-industrial Britain. Given the fact that peasants might not often have enjoyed an abundance of meat protein, then edibility, as well as the supposed economic threat posed by the badger, might have been factors limiting its population. The Forest Laws and sporting interest may not have been felt to be urgently relevant where this animal was involved. The badger was never really a noble quarry hence protection was unlikely to have been of general consequence.

However, that the badger survived extensively is an indisputable fact, and new tolerance and understanding together with recent legislation should ensure that it continues to be a generally common wild animal.

Whilst the national badger population has fallen somewhat in recent years there are areas as has been indicated where numbers have increased or remained substantial. A major reason for some setts remaining largely free from interference is that in recent years the conservation movement has gained momentum and the number of protected areas is increasing. The Nature Conservancy Council administers 135 nature reserves whilst other organisations, particularly the County Naturalists Trust, manage hundreds more. Badgers can be found in many such reserves. In addition as already stated, the Forestry Commission regards these animals with considerable approval.

I believe that the existence of national forestry has been one major factor allowing the increase in badger population in the 1950s and 1960s. Of course, the badger exists in privately owned areas but too often, even in recent years, experience in some of these has not been helpful to the species. I know of a number of such areas where there are few badgers even though the habitat could be regarded as ideal, mainly because of the conflict of sporting interests.

Increased knowledge has also helped to make clear the beneficial aspects of the badger's activities, as confirmed in a recent edition published by the Council for Nature and prepared by a Working Party appointed at a Conference convened by the Council, the Fauna Preservation Society and the Society for the Promotion of Nature Reserves. The late Professor H. R. Hewer, Chairman of the Council at that time, wrote in his preface to the booklet: 'Of all our animals, the mammalian predators are most in need of re-appraisal in the light of new knowledge about their role in nature and their place in the native fauna.' And the working party rightly concluded and made clear that in normal circumstances the badger does 'little harm and some good'. It was emphasised that 'only under exceptional circumstances do they need controlling'.

As for methods of badger-control the working party concluded that digging should only be conducted by skilled people under strict rules of procedure and not at all during the first five months of the year. Snaring was criticised as it could cause much suffering, whilst if the animal was to be trapped a strong cage was rightly said to be essential. They considered that shooting had the advantage of affording a selective approach.

The report emphasised that gas was illegal and that it should not be used against badgers. Gassing is permissible for the purposes of killing foxes, moles and rodents in their holes or burrows but not in order to destroy any other wild animal. Similarly the use of gin traps (or of any spring trap not approved by the Ministry of Agriculture) is illegal. This prohibition applied in Scotland from April 1973.

I am anxious about the suggestion that badgers can be controlled by shooting. Far too many ill-informed people use guns recklessly. I am obviously not referring to the organisations of shooting people who do much that is creditable but to the irresponsible minority, largely outside their influence. The recommendations of the Working Party with regard to firearms are that the minimum shot size suitable is AAA and this should only be fired at ranges of less than 25yd. The minimum size of rifle recommended is ·22 Hornet and such rifles should not be used at a range exceeding 50yd. Thankfully too, 'Air weapons are not considered to be suitable for use in predator control'.

Most predators remain outside protective legislation other than that afforded by the Protection of Animals Act 1911 which covers wild animals only when they are in captivity, the immunity applying only from the point when captivity commences. In many cases it might appear that no further protection is needed, yet the fairly general experience of the badger in recent years does point to the need for these matters to be kept under continuous review in order that adequate and timely protection can be afforded as and when necessary. Fortunately, the badger can now be described as a protected mammal even if the measures are necessarily incomplete.

A fitting comment upon recent change is provided by a new public house in Annesley Woodhouse, Notts, which bears the name 'The Badger Box'. Few people today understand its meaning. Writing in *The Victoria County History of Nottingham-*

shire in 1906, Prof J. W. Carr provided a brief account of the badger's position in the county, stating that badgers were caught nearly every winter at Annesley Park and inferring that these animals were used for baiting. Hopefully the last trace of the practice both in Nottinghamshire and in the rest of Britain might lie in the name of that new inn.

Yet there are still other more subtle dangers. A few years ago people were alarmed about the effect upon the badger of the ill-controlled use of insecticides and other chemicals in agriculture. Certainly in many areas the badger has been and is affected since it forms the end of a food-chain. Fortunately controls introduced since the mid-1960s have become rather more of a safeguard and a relevant scrutiny continues.

In a world short of food we cannot turn our backs upon the need for agricultural production and thus cannot easily condemn the use of applied science in controlling the ravages of natural pests and in expanding production. Those controls which have been introduced in Britain to offer protection to our environment and health are welcome in that they are now such as to appreciably limit the extremely unpleasant and excessive damage to our natural balance which was experienced in the days before we were made aware of the situation with publication of *The Silent Spring*.

The overwhelming impact of insecticides and other chemicals at that time is not even now completely realised. Before the late 1950s each year about three-quarters of our avian predators can be assumed to have been breeding. In the early 1960s probably not more than half that proportion of our hawks and less than one-tenth of our golden eagles reared young whilst not more than one-quarter of Britain's peregrine falcons were breeding. Since the populations of this falcon and of one or two other birds of prey were much below their pre-war levels a survival threat was obvious. At this time, too, it is thought that up to half the birds of prey which did lay eggs broke them, for one alarming effect of the new chemicals was to lead to a severe weakening of the shell.

Animals were annihilated, too. It is difficult to be certain about the precise effect of the new poisons upon badgers in the first years of the 1960s but it is likely to have been extensive, as it was for other mammals at the end of food-chains. B. Vesey Fitzgerald, in his book *The Vanishing Wildlife of Britain*, has described the 'fox death' of 1959–60 when over 1,300 foxes were found dead in East Anglia, which he attributed mainly to the extensive use of dieldrin. The recent latest restrictions upon this poison have come not before time.

Vesey Fitzgerald also described the use of herbicides on road verges as of significant harmfulness. I suppose that local authorities and other bodies concerned with highways have to be alert to the cause of public economy, but hope that more authorities will pursue the longer vision of those enlightened ones which rely more upon manual tidying than chemical spray.

The dangers are real in all aspects of nature. Too often water has been polluted by pesticides and similar dangerous substances carried in natural drainage, entering streams sometimes through thoughtlessness or error. As a result, rivers, then the seas and oceans have received much harmful and alien content. Since many of these substances are often most persistent their effect may not be yet concluded. The main needs now are for continued vigilance upon an international scale, for ever-effective and relevant scrutiny and for sanction to prevent the damage of negligence and short-sighted policies.

The removal of hedges has, in many areas, gone too far already for the hedgerows of Britain are reservoirs of life and stores of sustenance for nature. There seems no good reason to give grants for further hedgerow removal. Not all the occupants of our hedgerows are harmful to man's interest. It is all very well for a wiser and modern Britain to cater for natural recreation and to allow developments like national parks, as provided by the Countryside Acts, but great acreages without a hedge in sight are utterly devoted to intensive agriculture where there is no scope for the co-existence of natural life.

Obviously there is a dilemma. The world is changing. Areas

which have supplied Britain and Western Europe with relatively cheap food and raw materials are less able or willing to do so. We have, therefore, to provide more for ourselves, but for what are we growing? Growth is desirable to enrich the quality of life but increasing numbers of people have begun to consider that a life barren of natural contact and variety would be a badly impoverished one. Growth has meant increased comfort and greater humanity but it should not mean that man is restricted to a future of natural sterility confined within a narrow urban conformity.

There must be balance. We do need to grow food and produce timber. Fortunately many of those who are directly involved in this production are more aware than the rest of us of the dangers of any policy of too narrow an accountancy. They are aware, too, that nature is often a little more adaptable than man may frequently assume. They are aware that Britain's countryside has been shaped by man; that our rural charm is often designed rather than accidental. There is, then, no absolute justification for the most dismal pessimism. Anxiety remains, but not so profoundly as some seem to accept, for the worst of our myopia may be over.

Such a view is based, soundly, upon the realisation that we ourselves are part of a complicated natural system and, whilst we have interfered with this system and within this system, it is one which in the end we cannot or must not overthrow. Obviously, for centuries, man has changed his environment, the massive effect of the English enclosures more than illustrate this. However, natural variety must remain part of our heritage for it may provide a greater health than anything we may devise. This certainly does not mean that change is precluded for there is little general reason to insist that all change is entirely insensitive and intolerant just as there is no reason to presume that the adaptability of nature has reached its limit. We should not assume too little but at the same time we should not require that adaptability to be overstrained, for the tensions thus created, and reflected within ourselves, are not always such as

I   133

can desirably be sustained. Thus, if animal life is found horrid, then eventually we must deplore our own existence.

This attitude suggests neither a vegetarian nor a long-suffering approach. Conservation certainly does not mean that man's interests are utterly ignored, merely that a broader and longer interest is served. There are times when, despite this wider concern, animal life must be controlled. In certain circumstances then it may be essential that badgers, like other animals, should be destroyed or removed from a particular territory.

Some of those who criticised the 1973 Badgers Act for not going far enough demanded that absolute protection should be enacted. This is scarcely practicable. If it is proved that a badger is diseased and that the disease is harmful to its own or to other species then destruction cannot be condemned. If it is clear that development is in the public interest and that a sett stands in the path of the development, then it may be appropriate for the badgers to be removed. Both the removal and any essential destruction should be carried out in a humane manner.

The Report of the Universities Federation for Animal Welfare for 1972–3 states that a more than fair measure of success has attended its practice and sponsorship of humane methods of capturing wild badgers. These avoid the use of tongs, terriers or digging. The report comments that patience and skill are essential and this is illustrated by the account of the removal of badgers from a sett in Dursley, Gloucestershire. Part of the sett which lay under a building site was destroyed. The rest was under the gardens of two private houses and the owners of these co-operated in the attempt to capture the remaining badgers, one boar having previously been removed. Eventually three badgers were taken in a baited box trap and the following evening they were freed in the large Buckinghamshire wood in which the first captive had been released.

Following this humane example, the Frodsham Natural History Society reported that it had acted as an 'adoption agency' for ten badgers, linking up those areas with unwanted cubs or adults to people wishing to repopulate their areas.[8]

Rightly this society insists that it will only help place badgers in the wild and only where they can be rehabilitated.

As badger numbers recover we might expect increasing numbers to be killed on the highway although the animals have proved most adaptable to new roads in some areas. It is fortunate that the badger possesses this adaptability for we have already seen several species of predator either disappear from these islands or become exceedingly rare. The wild cat, the polecat and the pine marten were killed off in England during the last century and restricted to the remote fastnesses now occupied. They were trapped and poisoned, shot and snared, and no doubt many were stuffed and put into glass cases upon Victorian and Edwardian mantelpieces. Sadly, this fashion may not be entirely finished for a recent taxidermist's advertisement offered 'wild cat £15, badger £20, fox £15, raven £7 and kestrel £6'.

There would have been little excuse if we had permitted the recent severe decline in badger numbers to continue and, inevitably, to accelerate. Relatively few people had fully realised the overall position but they could rely, at least as far as badgers are involved, upon the greater concern of the interested thousands and the massive support which the cause of many wild creatures can now command.

Unhappily, the existence of protective law is no guarantee against unnecessary persecution. The Protection of Birds Act, for example, has been of great help but it is not of complete effect. Between January 1971 and August 1972 the Royal Society for the Protection of Birds received reports of 106 cases of persecution of birds of prey. Pole-traps had certainly been used in 66 of these cases. In the eighteen months involved it is certain that pole-traps were used on estates or farms in ten counties. Among the avian predators taken in these traps were buzzards, merlin, kestrels, sparrow hawks, little owls, tawny owls, and short-eared owls. There were other persecutions, too, but very few convictions were secured.

So we cannot rely upon law alone. Fortunately the growing

numbers of interested observers may provide an increasing level of watchfulness and persecution may be more likely to be detected and discouraged. The rural areas are more accessible and they are changing, too. When more primitive agricultural practices prevailed then economic threat from neighbouring badgers could not have been equably risked. Today, though, practices have changed and the more ancient economic dependences are over. Generally chickens, for example, are rather more securely kept.

Gradually, knowledge of the badger is accumulating. It is not yet complete. Much has been learned in the last twenty years and a great deal of information is now being compiled but there is more to learn, not least about breeding activity, family relationships and territorial activity. What we do know emphasises the usefulness as well as the fascination of this attractive mammal.

As much as any of our wild creatures, and indeed more than most, the badger today is viewed in a way which clearly illustrates our changing attitudes. More knowledge is coupled with a growing and generally justified humanity. Unfortunately the time of expansion in the national badger population had ended by 1970. I hope that improvement and recovery as a result of the amalgamation of conservational arrangement, improved attitudes and helpful legislation will now occur. This can only enhance the richness and diversity of our natural heritage in many areas where it is lacking abundance.

The assault on pollution may have far to go, the cause of conservation long to run, the pillaging of the profiteer still needing to be more firmly resisted, but progress in developing the necessary protection of society and in maintaining a healthy pace of environmental progress and natural conservation has been achieved. Brock can be proud of having contributed in no small way to this progress.

THE PROTECTION OF BADGERS

PASSING OF THE BILL

During 1972 reports of badger persecution from many parts of Britain were alarming. In some areas of Cheshire the onslaught was vicious and a vigilante patrol was operated and a badger society formed in the Frodsham area. Those responsible commenced duplication of a newsletter which reflected not only the position of the badger in the immediate locality but also further afield. Evidence of illegal action was collected from many areas and the extensive information obtained justified concern and political consideration. By the autumn of that year many Mammal Society recorders were noting the grim effect of persecution which, added to the casualties of economic change and from modern transportation, made it clear that a measure of protection had become necessary.

It was at this point that I decided upon action to provide for adequate badger protection and, being unsuccessful in any attempt to present a Private Members' Bill, I decided to attempt a Bill under the Ten Minute Rule. Such Bills have little chance of enactment, but I was anxious to achieve more than publicity alone. The opportunity to present the Ten Minute Rule Bill came on Wednesday, 14 February, after I had submitted a statement as to the purposes of the Bill submitted and I secured other sponsors from both sides of the House: Mr Peter Archer QC, Mr Joe Ashton, Mr Sidney Chapman, Mr David Clark, Mr Eric Cockeram, Mr Terry Davies, Mr David James, Mr Brynmor John, Mr Cecil Parkinson, Mr William Price, and Sir John Rogers.

As most Private Members' Bills can be defeated by just one disapproving Member it was decided to submit proposals which appeared somewhat narrow in scope. I proposed therefore that it should be an offence for badgers to be killed or taken, or for there to be an attempt to kill or take badgers on land without the prior written permission of the owner of the land. This was in fact much less narrow than it appeared, for in most areas persecution usually involved trespassing.

Before presentation I discussed my Bill with the Earl of Arran who had just presented his Bill to protect badgers in the Upper House. Whilst I thought his Bill better in purpose and more desirable in general content than my own in that it was more comprehensive, I did not feel that it would succeed in its existing form and thus it had little chance in the Commons.

As foreseen there was no opposition to the presentation of my Bill on 14 February. Second Reading was given nine days later and the Bill was then added to the list. Fortunately it seemed early enough in the session for the Bill to have a real chance of enactment.

By now the Bill had aroused a lot of interest and there was much publicity. At this time there was encouragement from the actions of the Forestry Commission which had recently obtained its relevant and helpful bye-laws. Action was taken under these against three diggers who were convicted.

The majority of my mail was favourable although I received

some criticism after Lord Arran's proposals secured Second Reading in the Lords. Much of that criticism was based upon an inability to perceive that a modest step forward was better than none.

Much was done however to clarify Lord Arran's Bill at Committee Stage. During Report Stage amendments designed to make for conservational and legal soundness were accepted, and Third Reading was later proposed. Immediately following this, Lord Arran brought the Bill across to the Commons where I presented it. It was this Bill then which went before the Standing Committee, a Committee which began business at 10.30 am and rose, its task completed, at 11.08 am, having dealt with 13 amendments.

Report Stage and Third Reading were set down on the last day for Private Members' business, 20 July. Badgers were indeed fortunate that their Bill went through without objection and the Royal Assent was given shortly afterwards.

PROVISIONS OF THE ACT

The Act makes it an offence, maximum penalty £100 per badger involved, to wilfully kill, injure or take, or to attempt to kill, injure or take any badger, or for a person to have in his possession a recently killed badger or the pelt from a freshly killed animal. It is not an offence for an authorised person to control badgers providing control is not exercised in a prohibited way. An authorised person is the owner or occupier of land or their servant or the servant of the local authority, the Nature Conservancy, the Ministry of Agriculture, Fisheries and Food or the Secretary of State for Scotland.

Protection is taken further in those places which may be established as areas for the special protection of badgers (by order of the Secretary of State). Land of this kind will first be recommended to the Minister by the Nature Conservancy Council and any Order implementing such recommendation is subject to annulment by either House of Parliament. In an area of special protection, action to destroy or take badgers is an offence unless it is necessary to prevent disease or serious damage to property.

Both within and outside special protection areas it is now an offence to use badger tongs or to shoot at badgers with unsuitable firearms. A shot-gun must not be less than 20 bore and a rifled weapon should not use a bullet of less than 38 grains discharged at a force of less than 160 foot pounds.

It is an offence to own, control or offer for sale any badger unless a licence has been granted by the Nature Conservancy Council. This body may also grant licences for the tagging or marking of badgers; otherwise the use of any marking device is illegal. People found to be offending under the Act who refuse to quit land or to give their name and address when asked by a police officer or an authorised person, can be fined up to £20. In addition to any fines imposed the courts may order the forfeiture of any weapon or article used in committing the offence.

The Act thus represents a very considerable measure of security for the species. Certainly, the capture of cubs for sale as pets is now illegal and digging by trespassers is entirely prohibited. Added to the protection afforded by previous legislation which forbids the use of spring traps, gas or poison against badgers it may be fair to assume that the badger now benefits from the maximum possible enforceable provision.

REFERENCES

1 Baily's *Magazine* (1880)
2 Batten, H. Mortimer. *The Badger Afield and Underground* (Witherby, 1923)
3 Bryden, H. A. *Nature and Sport in Great Britain* (1904)
4 Cocks, A. H. *The Victoria County History of Buckinghamshire*, vol 1 (London, 1905)
5 Cox, Nicholas. *The Gentleman's Recreation* (London, 1677)
6 Drabble, Philip. *Badger at my Window* (London, 1959)
7 Fitter, Richard. *The Ark in our Midst* (London, 1972)
8 The Frodsham Natural History Society. 'Badger Review' (December, 1973)
9 Gill, E. L. *The Victoria County History of Durham*, vol 1 (London, 1905)
10 Hansard. 'Report of the Standing Committee considering the Badger Bill' (July, 1973)
11 Harting, J. E. *The Badger*, Zoologist Series 3 (1888)
12 Jefferies, Richard. *The Gamekeeper at Home* (1878)
13 ——. *The Story of my Heart* (London, 1883)
14 Killingley, A. in *The Countryman* (Spring/Summer, 1973)

15 King, H. H. 'Working Terriers, Badgers and Badger-Digging', *The Field* (1931)

16 The Mammal Society. The National Badger Survey, *The Mammal Review*, vol 2, no 2 (1972)

17 Millais, J. G. *Mammals of Great Britain and Ireland*, vol 2 (1904)

18 Muirhead, R. H. 'Bovine Tuberculosis in Wild Badgers', *State Veterinary Journal* (September, 1972)

19 Neal, Dr Ernest. *The Badger* (London, 1948, reprinted 1971)

20 Nimrod. *The Life of a Sportsman* (London, 1842)

21 Paget, Dr Richard. 'A Case of Osteomyelitis', The Zoological Society of London (1972)

22 Paterson, J. *The Gestation of the Badger*, Zoologist Series 3 (1904)

23 Pearsall, W. H. *Mountain and Moorland* (London, 1950)

24 Pease, Sir Alfred. *The Badger* (1898)

25 Pease, Sir Alfred and Blakeborough, J. Fairfax. *The Life and Habits of the Badger* (1914)

26 Shepherd, Mrs S. *Brocky* (London, 1964)

27 Southwell, T. *The Victoria County History of Norfolk*, vol 1 (London, 1904)

28 *The Sporting Magazine* (1800)

29 Swayne, R. A. *The Victoria County History of Herefordshire*, vol 1 (London, 1908)

30 Turberville, G. *The Noble Art of Venerie* (1576, new edition, 1908)

31 Whall, T. J. 'Badger Notes', *Survey of Leicestershire Natural History* (1963)

32 Wilson, J. F. *The Badgers of Cliff Wood, High Melton*, unpublished thesis, Doncaster College of Education (1972)

33 Vyner, R. T. *Notitia Venatica* (London, 1841)

ACKNOWLEDGEMENTS

I am grateful to a large number of people including naturalists and not a few politicians who are interested in the fauna of Great Britain. To all these, my thanks. Whilst a list of such individuals would be too long to appear here I must record my appreciation of the work done and the help given during the Parliamentary session 1972–3 by Dr Ernest Neal, and my gratitude to Dr Richard Paget for his advice, photographs and, especially, for his care of our Rother Valley setts.

I am indebted too to Mr Derek Warren, the Nottinghamshire County Badger Recorder, for photographs and information concerning persecution in that county and to Messrs Neil Clark and Geoffrey N. Wright for photographs. I am also grateful to the London Zoo for permission to reproduce the photograph of the hog badger.

Gratitude is due to my dentist, a most knowledgeable naturalist, J. S. Griffith of Conisbrough and to Mr B. Smith, my informant from the Doncaster College of Education, High Melton.

I should like to express appreciation of publicity given to my work for badgers by the local newspapers of my area. The *South Yorkshire Times* was most helpful through its editor Dick Ridyard and Bryan Longworth, the senior reporter for the Sheffield area. The *Sheffield Star*, the *Worksop Guardian* and the *Rotherham Advertiser* were extremely kind, too. I also welcomed the opportunity to contribute an article about the need for badger conservation to *The Field* and I am grateful to the magazine's editor, Wilson Stephens, for his support and commendation.

I was pleased to have the support of members of my own constituency party, including my agent Friend Cooper, a formidable figure in South Yorkshire politics.

Lastly, my deepest gratitude is owed to my wife, Margaret, for her help and advice and, with Mrs Irene Hartley, for the typing. The comment that a Member's wife does not enjoy the easiest of lives must be a dreadful understatement.

INDEX

Agriculture, Ministry of, 66, 71, 72, 130

American badger, 87

Argyllshire, 103

Ayrshire, 103

Badger, appearance, 14-17; coloration, 17-18; dentition, 21-2, 52; diet, 54-70; names, 16, 102; population, 97-101; reproduction, 40, 49-50; senses, 23; sounds, 33-4

Badgers Act, 10, 30, 71, 99, 113, 115, 134

Badger Survey, 78, 80, 94, 97

Batten, H. Mortimer, 20, 40, 44, 56, 59, 60, 67, 76, 110

Blakeborough, J. Fairfax, 59, 103, 104, 106

Bloomfield, A., 48

Buckinghamshire, 114

Carr, Prof J. W., 131

Chalmers, Patrick, 115

Cheshire, 110

Clare, John, 115

Clark, Neil, 54

Cocks, A. H., 114

Cornwall, 71, 91

Council for Nature, 129

Cox, N., 106

Cumberland, 111

Denbigh, 91

Devon, 100

Dogs, 19

Doncaster College of Education, 97

Dorset, 103

Drabble, P., 66, 96

Durham, 111

Fauna Preservation Society, 129

Ferret badger, 88

Fitter, R., 95

Fitzgerald, B. Vesey, 132

145

Forestry Commission, 10, 93, 129
Frodsham Natural History Society, 134

Gill, E. L., 111
Glen Garry, 92
Gloucestershire, 71, 72, 94, 100, 103
Griffith, J. S., 46

Hampshire, 103
Hardy, Mrs M. A., 120
Harting, J. E., 114
Hertfordshire, 110
Hewer, Prof H. R., 129
Hobday, Sir F., 68
Hog badger, 88
House of Commons, 10

Jefferies, Richard, 54, 70, 126

Kent, 91, 103
Killingley, A., 35, 67
King, H. H., 110, 113

Lancum, H., 66
Lincolnshire, 103
London, 92

Macaulay, T. B., 106
Macpherson, Rev H. A., 95
Mammal Society, 35, 67, 78, 79, 94, 99, 113
Masson, E. le, 109, 110
Millais, J. G., 110
Moyle, Roland, 72
Muirhead, R. H., 71

Nature Conservancy Council, 129
Neal, Dr E., 17, 18, 33, 50, 56, 66, 68, 84
Norfolk, 111
Northamptonshire, 103

Nottinghamshire, 130-1

Paget, Dr R. J., 55, 68
Parliament, 30, 55
Paterson, J., 114, 115
Pearsall, W. H., 92
Pease, Sir A., 103, 106, 109, 111, 113, 114
Phillpotts, E., 115
Pitt, Miss F., 68
Pole traps, 135
Protection of Animals Act (1911), 130
Protection of Birds Acts, 135

Ratel, 88
Renfrewshire, 103
Ross, 103
Rother Valley, 9
Royal Society for the Protection of Animals, 97
Royal Society for the Protection of Birds, 135

Salvin, F. H., 114
Scotland, 81, 92, 99, 109
Scott, Sir P., 110
Shepherd, Mrs S., 17-18
Shropshire, 103
Society for the Promotion of Nature Reserves, 129
Somerset, 81, 84, 103
Southwell, T., 111
Staffordshire, 97, 98, 103
Suffolk, 103
Surrey, 92, 103
Sussex, 92, 93, 94

Teledu, 88
Turberville, G., 18, 86

University Federation for Animal Welfare, 134

Vyner, R. T., 103

Wales, 56, 60, 81, 91, 109, 113
Waterhouse, M., 97
Whall, T. J., 30

Williamson, H., 115
Wilson, J. F., 29
Wordsworth, W., 13

Yorkshire, 9, 20, 55, 76, 79, 92, 94, 99, 103, 110, 121, 126